Mastering

Your Seasons

Lisa L. Schwarz

Dedication

I want to thank my husband, Brad, for walking with me through 25 years of various seasons of life. We have laughed, we have cried, we have agreed and we have disagreed. We have celebrated, we have mourned, we have gotten along, and we have fought. From the birth of our six children to dropping them off at college, from being a stay at home mom to being the founder of a ministry, I have found companionship with Brad. Many thanks to him for his partnership and support in all I do and for never giving up on me or letting me give up on my dreams or myself.

Life is good, babe and I love you more today than the day I married you. I did, I still do, and I always will. #partnership #tobeloved

I would be remiss if I did not also acknowledge my mentor of 21 years, Kate Megill, who has taught me how to walk in the Word through every season of life. She has loved me soft, and she has loved me hard. But through it all she has encouraged me that every season is moving me up to a new level with God. The spiral staircase is inspired by her continual reminders that, with God, we never plummet downward, but rather we always cycle upward.

Kate, you are truly a picture of His love. Thank you for sharpening me and for always expecting more out of me. #discipleship

Contents

Prayer Practices

Throughout my years of ministering, counseling, and discipling, I have discovered that many people don't understand how to declare God's Truths into their lives through prayer. We know what it means to ask God for things and to supplicate, but we struggle when it comes to standing firmly on His biblical promises and principles. I've spent many years trying to tell people what it meant, but over the past five years, I have found it more effective to simply demonstrate it.

When the disciples asked Jesus to teach them how to pray, He responded by demonstrating.

> "One day Jesus was praying in a certain place. When he finished, one of his disciples said to him, "Lord, teach us to pray, just as John taught his disciples." 2 He said to them, "When you pray, say: "'Father, hallowed be your name, your kingdom come. 3 Give us each day our daily bread. 4 Forgive us our sins, for we also forgive everyone who sins against us. And lead us not into temptation.'"
>
> Luke 11:1-4

We see examples of Jesus teaching by demonstrating throughout the Scriptures. I offer a time once a week in my office called "Prayer Observatory." In this "class" I simply open up my prayer time and communion with the Lord for observation. I act as if no one else is in the room, and I interact with God as I would any other morning, which is typically pretty verbal. It is *not* so that others would see my prayer life, trust me, it is vulnerable and often feels invasive, but rather I do this so others can learn by seeing. I have had great responses from people throughout the years in regard to the observatory and many have shared specifically how the opportunity to observe has profoundly affected their own communion with God.

It is for this purpose that I have included the "Prayer Practices" in this book. They are like "mini observatories" captured on paper for you. My desire is to demonstrate what it looks like to take a biblical principle and declare it through prayer, thus teaching you how to pray with **authority** and **confidence**. I hope you find them helpful and challenging, and I pray that you will be empowered by them.

Introduction

I have spoken at many conferences and retreats over the years, most of them for women or youth-aged girls, and throughout them all I have seen a recurring truth. Everyone walks through different seasons of life, and these seasons are not tied to your age. Meaning, seasons are about much *more* than just your age. And although we often depict the concept of seasons into ages, or chronological stages encountered through life, this does not completely capture the fullness of how God defines seasons of life.

Recently, I was asked to speak at a conference entitled "Seasons of Life" for a women's group in Missouri. Women of all ages would be in attendance, and it was inferred that they wanted a message to speak to every generation, or "season of life." Because I love the concept of discipleship and the older teaching the younger, I was anxious to get started on developing my material. But as I prayed about how the Lord wanted me to move forward with the message, I began to realize that seasons of life have really nothing to do with age, but rather the events, or happenings, of your life. Furthermore, in those seasons of events or happenings, there are spiritual happenings taking place as well. As much as I tried to stay focused on bringing the message they were looking for, I could not help but go where God was leading me. So instead of writing about motherhood, or mid-life challenges, or the empty nest syndrome, I was drawn to focus on spiritual seasons that we cycle through in the midst of our circumstances.

As I pressed into this concept through prayer, God showed me the richness of what He wants to teach us through creation and HIS seasons. In every natural event, there is a spiritual "happening" taking place. The reality is, there are times or seasons in life. This is part of God's creation. It is the natural cycle of life, and nothing we can do will stop this cycle. However, I believe it is important that we learn to look past our natural circumstance and our natural season and recognize what God is doing in the spirit. Throughout the gospels, Jesus uses natural things as a frame of reference to describe things in the spirit. He connects the dots from the natural to the spiritual by giving us something our brain can connect to. This enables us to comprehend an "unexplainable concept." Ultimately, His desire is to draw the heart and mind of His listeners beyond the natural and into the spiritual. It is important that we learn from this example and consider that God still wants to teach us and show us spiritual things through the natural.

I am continuously learning that a huge part of walking victoriously is allowing the Holy Spirit to show me beyond just what I see and experience on the left and the right. The reality is, you are a spiritual being having a human experience. You must learn to think beyond being a human being having a spiritual experience. When you purposefully step outside of the natural world and into the spirit and gain His insight to His purpose in all things, then you will learn to master the seasons of life.

1 For Such a Time as This

To everything there is a season, A time for every purpose under heaven; A time to be born, And a time to die; A time to plant, And a time to pluck what is planted. A time to kill, And a time to heal; A time to break down, And a time to build up; A time to weep, And a time to laugh; A time to mourn, And a time to dance; A time to cast away stones, And a time to gather stones; A time to embrace, And a time to refrain from embracing; A time to gain, And a time to lose; A time to keep, And a time to throw away; A time to tear, And a time to sew; A time to keep silence, And a time to speak; A time to love, And a time to hate; A time of war, And a time of peace.

Ecclesiastes 3:1-8

THE CONCEPT OF TIME

Time is a puzzling concept for humans. We have defined or narrowed the idea of time down to what is represented on a watch or a calendar, and everything we do often centers around those two things. But we must try and understand: God is not limited by time as we know it. He is outside of time. Think with me back to creation. The finale of creation was the creation of man and woman on day six. On all the days leading up to day six, God set the stage for us, the main characters who would live within the plot of His story. On day one, God created day and night. He created the time parameters that man and woman would dwell within. The point is: God is not bound by time as we are, nor is He controlled by chronological time as we know it.

And He said to them, "It is not for you to know times or seasons which The Father has put in His own authority."

Acts 1:7

The above verse quotes Jesus' response to a question

3

regarding the timing of the restoration of the kingdom of Israel. He does so by reminding His audience that the timing of the Lord cannot be measured or calculated on a worldly timetable. In other words, they wanted Him to answer a kingdom matter question with earthly terms. The kingdom and the work of the kingdom is spiritual in its character and cannot be measured on an earthly scale.

Acts 1:7 presents two different meanings for the word *time.* The word *times* comes from the Greek word *chronos,* which means, "a duration of time which may be a point, a lapse, a span, a period, a measure, a length or succession of time." This is the time tracked by a calendar or a watch. It is the linear time that we function within here on earth and moves chronologically. There is nothing we can do to stop *chronos* times. It is the sequential time that God created on day one.

But the word *seasons* used in Acts 1:7 comes from the Greek word *kairos.* This word suggests a KIND of time, a time of special happenings occurring within the time frame of chronological time (chronos). It also denotes the importance of performing a task, or an intentional yet limited time of opportunity, meaning "now" is the time for something specific. Kairos timing is of the spirit and although it functions within the linear, it is not bound by nor is it limited to the linear. We might think of kairos as a cluster of occurrences that God strategically orchestrates. It is a time of opportunity in the spirit. Perhaps you might say it is a "favorable moment."

Consider the phrase that we often hear quoted from the book of Esther:

> *"For if you remain completely silent at this time, relief and deliverance will arise for the Jews from another place, but you and your father's house will perish. Yet who knows whether you have come to the kingdom **for such a time as this**?"*
> Esther 4:14
> (emphasis mine)

The word *time* in this verse comes from the Hebrew word *eth,* which denotes the idea of "an event; experiences, fortunes; occurrence or occasion." It is reflective of a kairos time. In other words, the timing of the Lord was *now* and although it was taking place within natural linear time, it was not a chronological thing, rather more about the series of events and cluster of occurrences. God had been working up to that moment for years. On the day of Esther's birth, the Lord was aware of this "now" moment. All things leading up to that moment were intentionally setting the stage for the rescue of the Jews through Esther. This was the moment God had been preparing for!

> *"Remember the former things of old, For I am God, and there is no other; For I am God, and there is none like Me; Declaring the end from the beginning, And from ancient times things that are not yet done, Saying my counsel shall stand, And I will do all My pleasure."*
>
> *Isaiah 46:9-10*

Isaiah reminds us that from the very beginning of time as we know it, God has been working to accomplish a greater cause and fulfill a greater purpose. In other words, our God knows the end from the beginning and it is His heart to work all things out in our lives to bring us into that end. He invites us in to play a part in His plan. However, kingdom timing is of the essence when bringing the will and work of God into fruition. It is so important that we learn to trust God and His timing, which He monitors through our events and happenings. That is how He sets the pace. When we truly understand that His heart and His desire is to weave us into His plan for His kingdom, it will change everything about how we view our lives. This captures the depths of Romans 8:28:

> *"And we know that all things work together for good to those who love God, to those who are the called according to His purpose."*

To *know* means to "perceive or gain understanding or knowledge." It means we do not simply know the words in this verse, but we agree with them and allow the truth of them to manifest in our thoughts, attitudes, and actions. It is a truth that permeates and supersedes what we see or the facts of our circumstances, because we know that we know God is

5

accomplishing a greater purpose in all things. That means ALL things. Not some things, but ALL things. There is nothing excluded from the word "all" and we must take it at its word in our lives. I want to take this verse off the page of my Bible and ingest it and make it a part of who I am, thus declaring it daily!

PRAYER PRACTICE

Father, ALL things in MY life ARE working together... being weaved and intertwined in and out of the events of my life for good and with good godly intent, because I love You, God and I AM called for a purpose that You are bringing me into!
Amen and amen in the name of Jesus.

Notice in the Romans 28 verse that it is according to HIS purpose, not ours. Therein lies another challenge. The challenge is for us to let go of our ideas and expectations in every occurrence, and surrender so that God's will and purpose could come to pass. The word *purpose* means to "set forth or place before; to purpose, determine." Meaning there is a determined course for your life that lies ahead of you. It is set forth in motion and it is the finger of God that draws you into the rivet of His path. We often spend so much time trying to figure all things out and how we think they should go or what "needs to happen," that we often end up manipulating or distorting the finger of God.

An example of this is found in Genesis. God promised the birth of a son to Abraham. Abraham and Sarah, in their impatience, attempt to force God's will to come to fruition by birthing a son, Ishmael, through Sarah's maid servant, Hagar. Unfortunately they looked at the promise of God through their natural eyes and missed out on understanding the importance of spiritual timing. I have often done this myself in my own life or in my ministry. There have been times when I have known what God is saying or that He has clearly promised something or made something clear, yet I immediately begin to force the timing of that thing. Instead of waiting on the ease of the Isaac, I forced an Ishmael to come forth. All that came from that was chaos and dissention. It was hard and not easy because it was not the yoke of the Lord (Matt. 11:28). Note

6

that although man cannot thwart the will of God, we can certainly mess up the plan in which we come into His will. This is often because of our inability to understand we must wait on God's timing. Our tactics, even though often innocent, can manipulate and distort the path of our lives, making it twisted and challenging instead of easy and light!

In Genesis 18, after God has cleaned up the mess that Abraham and Sarah created through their attempt to hasten His timing, God says this in verse 14:

> *"Is anything too hard for the Lord? At the appointed time I will return to you, according to the time of life, and Sarah shall have a son."*
>
> *Genesis 18:14*

Oh, what a God we serve and how beautiful is His rebuke and reminder that nothing is too hard for Him! He appoints time in our lives perfectly... never a minute early and never a minute late. He has a final plan and purpose that He continually brings us into, and that plan is of a spiritual nature. It is spiritual work for a much higher purpose than we can even begin to fathom. "According to the time of life" means at the time of birth, it will happen. I find it interesting how we live in a culture where it is popular for women and doctors to choose the dates of the births of their babies for the sake of convenience. We have become so adept at controlling all things in order to live more predictable lives. This has only proven to feed our need for control and ultimately squelches the practice of faith and trusting God.

We have lost our ability to wait and suffer long. Instead we would rather pop things in the microwave for a quick return. In doing so, we miss out on the tenderness and flavor of that which we are eating. Waiting for the appointed time is an acquired taste. It requires an eternal perspective on timing and the importance of not forcing or manipulating God's timing.

In John 2:4, we get a glimpse of Jesus as He wrestles with chronos time and kairos time.

> *"Woman, what does your concern have to do with me? My hour has not yet come."*

The word *hour* means a "certain definite time or a moment." What I see in this verse is that Jesus comes up against man's understanding of time. Jesus was not used to being bound by chronological time because He had always dwelt outside of time in the spirit realm. He had first-hand experience in the timings of God and the intentionality of occurrences and seasons. He had the wisdom and the knowledge of time in the spirit, yet now He was called to live and function within the natural linear time that we dwell within. In this passage, He was being asked to force God's hand to perform a miracle. We see here a warring between Jesus's Godness and humanness in regard to the whether or not His time had come.

Even Jesus had to balance the two concepts of time and be sensitive to stay focused on the fixed timings of the Lord. We must come to a place where we understand, as Jesus did, that there are fixed appointments in our lives and God lines up our occurrences *for such a time as this*! It is Him, ALL HIM, using everything in our lives to bring forth the fullness of life in us. It is His desire to perfect us and bring us into the fullness of His promises, and He does this by "aligning the stars" through our every day events. Don't discount the power of how He uses your circumstances to bring forth a greater plan.

In the following chapters, you will see how God uses the seasons of your life to grow you more deeply into Himself. It begins with the awareness that God will use the natural to reveal the spiritual to you.

LESSONS THROUGH NATURE

In His desire to connect with you, God reveals things through nature as a frame of reference to understand spiritual truths. He knows that in order for humans to comprehend things of a spiritual nature, He must use the things that we can see in this world. This is why Scripture compares kingdom concepts to a mustard seed, or a soldier, or a tree. He wants us to grasp these kingdom concepts and if we pay attention, we will see them displayed throughout nature. We must shift our understanding of nature and see God and His character in all of creation. We have been so trained to look at nature scientifically that we often miss the heart of God and what

He can teach us as the Creator.

TRANSFORMING THE SEASON

We can't change God's seasons; they are a part of life, just like they are a part of nature.

> *"While earth remains, seedtime and harvest, cold and heat, winter and summer, and day and night shall not cease."*
> *Genesis 8:22*

This is a biblical concept. Seasons and cycles are a part of creation and are how the Lord made creation to function, and until He tells them to stop, they will continue. Our job is to shift our thinking from our circumstances to the heart of God. This is how we transform the cycle.

Remember, you don't want to be stuck by looking at things only through a chronos view. You must look for the kairos activity. Although there is one thing happening in linear time, there is always something going on in the spirit as well. Always! While you can't break the natural cycle, you can change your understanding of the cycle.

> *"Set your mind on things above and not on earthly things."*
> *Colossians 3:2*

> *"For our light affliction, which is but for a moment is working for us a far more exceeding and eternal weight of glory, while we do not look at the things which are seen, but a the things which are not seen. For the things which are seen are temporary, but the things which are not seen are eternal."*
> *2 Corinthians 4:17-18*

These verses exhort us to keep an eternal perspective. It is the practice of choosing to shift and not focus on the natural or the here and now, but to look beyond and believe that God is always working, and He is good! They give a practical view of what it looks like to "no longer be conformed to the pattern of this world, but be transformed by the renewing of your mind" (Romans 12:2).

In Colossians 3:2 (on page 9), the word *mind* is often interpreted into the word *affection*, and the original Greek word used here is often interpreted into the word *attitude*. The mind and the heart (attitude) are both included. The word *set* is an action verb. It is on us to turn this Word into action by not just hearing but doing. (James 1:22). So you must choose to direct your mind's attention and your heart's affection on the heart and character of God and to have His attitude toward all things.

> *"Having the same attitude like that of Christ Jesus..."*
> *Philippians 2:5*

Interestingly, the Greek word for *attitude* Paul uses in this verse is the same Greek word used for the word *mind* in Colossians 3:2. Again stressing the *intentional* setting of your thoughts and affections on the things of God. It is the exercise of your thinking and the intentional direction of your feelings. This takes practice, practice, and more practice. But, practice makes perfect.

We will practice this concept by looking at each season through the eyes of God. I want you to be aware of the dangers and tendencies of each of them, and develop an understanding of how God desires to work in each season. We no longer want to define each season as the world would, but as God would.

When you can look into seasons with clear understanding and a total belief of God's heart, it will change the way you enter them and walk through them, thus mastering your seasons!

Part 1
Winter Season
There's a Feast in Your Famine

2 Redefining Winter

As I initially prepared this message for teaching at the conference, I assumed that of course I would start out with the season of spring. It makes sense. Spring represents new beginnings and is where life begins. But as I prayed through my message the week I was to deliver it, the Lord reminded me that His ways are not our ways. I got a strong sense that He wanted me to open with winter instead of spring. When I asked the Lord, "Why?" He quickly reminded me that spiritually, life begins at death.

CHARACTERISTICS OF WINTER

When the days become shorter and the temperature becomes cooler, we know that winter is upon us. There are no leaves on the trees, no flowers blooming, and no fruit being produced. They lay dormant and no life comes forth.

With this season comes colder temperatures that can make things more difficult to accomplish. The weather can tend to keep us from accomplishing our work. We stay in the house more, and sometimes we even get stuck in the house, breeding a season of low activity. It is typically characterized as a season of death or stagnancy... no life.

I grew up in the Midwest and our kids were born there, too. Midwest winters are long and harsh. They linger *for-ev-er* and by the end, it feels though spring will never come. Having six homeschooled kiddos at home, I got to experience the effects of the long winters. Being stuck in the house would cause us to go a little stir crazy and by the time March came around, we were ready to move beyond that season and get back outdoors.

We can liken this to those seasons of life where circumstantially we experience the same. A time where there seems to be nothing happening, and there is no activity, no production, and no fruit of our labor. A life season in which we feel very dry or even lost.

Spiritually, the winter season is often compared to being in a wilderness. The wilderness is a place of dryness. It is deserted, and there are no signs of life. It is parched and void of activity. But the one thing that depicts a wilderness best, and I believe is true of a winter season, is that there is not a clear path on which to travel. Picture the wilderness. When you are standing out in the middle of a desert, no matter which direction you turn, you see no clear path and therefore lack direction and have the feeling of being lost. This is often true of spiritual winter seasons.

Other imagery that depicts this feeling is to compare a winter season to a drought or a famine, a death or season of sorrow, or an ending to something. Those are not pleasurable experiences. They can be long, dark, harsh, and cold and leave you feeling lost and abandoned. The lack of productivity is discouraging and brings feelings of defeat. You may feel "stuck" in one place or in a holding pattern.

CONNECTING THE DOTS

In nature, we know that winter always precedes spring. Even in the dead of winter, you have confidence that spring is just around the corner. It will come. There is no question that within those dead branches, there is life. In fact, the term "dormant" is more commonly used instead of calling the trees "dead." There is a natural order that causes that plant or tree to grow and produce again. As such, we expect two things. One, that spring will indeed come, and two, that what appears dead will once again produce life. In fact, there will not only be life, but there will be an increase. More fruit, more leaves, more flowers, larger branches, and a thicker trunk.

The same is true of us spiritually. Just like a seed has the DNA in it to produce again, so do we. This was part of the original blessing that God spoke to man: "Be fruitful and multiply." God, in His love and compassion, allows seasons of winter in our lives, for the purpose of nurturing that seed and ultimately bringing forth more life! His goal is to bring you into your fullness and complete you.

Let's remember the concept of embracing God's perspective in all things. The world's view of death, or the end of things, is not God's view.

> *"Jesus says, 'Most assuredly, I say to you, unless a grain of wheat falls into the ground and dies, it remains alone; but if it dies, it produces much grain.'"*
>
> *John 12:24*

> *"Foolish one, what you sow is not made alive unless it dies."*
>
> *1 Corinthians 15:36*

Jesus uses the law of creation to show the power death has to bring forth life. He presents a paradigm shift to His listeners and to us. The world tells us that death is an end, a stopping of life, no more productivity. Even though we have not yet actually experienced physical death, we can all relate to seasons of futility and low productivity; times when we feel like we are working for nothing and we see no fruit to our laboring. But according to what Jesus taught, we can stand on the truth that in the midst of that season, God is working to increase us!

❧ PRAYER PRACTICE

> *Father, I am in a season where I see no outcome, I am tired, weary, and I feel discouraged. But despite what I see and how I feel, I know what Your Word says... and if Your Word says it, I believe it. So, in Jesus' name, I declare and decree that in the midst of this season, You are working to produce much*

"grain" in and through my life. I agree and walk in Your truth and thank You for increasing me and the fruit of my labor. In Jesus' name, Amen.

LIFE-DEATH PRINCIPLE

Just like in creation, life *always* emerges from death. This is a promise we can stand on in our season of winter. It is a principle we see repeated throughout scripture. We can, and should, *expect* life. We should *expect* fruit to burst out of that place of winter. When we allow this truth to sear our souls, we need not dread or fear our winter's season, but rather, we can attack it head on!

Consider the process a seed goes through. In fact, let's pretend we are seeds for a moment. A seed is buried in the ground and left there, covered by the dirt, unseen and in the dark. Have you pictured it? Come on now, let this resonate with your life personally! Many pass by the seed and are never even aware of the seed's existence. They totally dismiss it. Only the farmer knows of the seed and its whereabouts because he is the one who planted the seed. He was intentional in where and when and how deep he planted it. He knows the DNA of the seed and knows the conditions the seed needs to bring forth life. He also knows what plant will come forth from that seed and knows what that plant needs in order to thrive. He knows the future potential of the seed and as such, he sets it up to succeed and prosper in a place with the perfect amount of light and shade and just the right climate. Before long, roots emerge from the seed, though still unseen, but soon, the seed ceases to be and it dies. Life and fruit overtake the seed. In other words, death is swallowed up by life! The seed gives up its life for a great production, and frankly for the purpose of multiplication. We know that not just fruit comes forth, but more seeds come out of that fruit.

You see, what the entire world misses, God sees. Just like the farmer, He is working underground in your life. He knows when to "bury" you, how deep to "bury" you and where to "bury" you. He is intentional and He has one purpose, and that is to bring forth the fruit of HIS DNA within you. He created you to be fruitful and multiply (Genesis 1:28), and it is the Father's perfect will to bring

14

you to that place.

> *"My Well-beloved has a vineyard on a very fruitful hill. He dug it up and cleared out its stones, and planted it with the choicest vine. He built a tower in its midst, and also made a winepress in it; So He expected it to bring forth good grapes."*
>
> *Isaiah 5:1&2*

Believe it or not, God is for you, even in your seasons of winter and He is setting you up to bring forth GOOD grapes!

℘ PRAYER PRACTICE

> *God, I praise you that You call me a fruitful vineyard and that You have set me up to bear fruit and to be successful and productive. I recognize that You have intentionally and strategically planted me where I can prosper and grow. I thank You Lord, that no matter what I see, I can stand upon this truth in my life. Your Word promises that I am empowered to flourish, and if Your Word says it, I believe it! So in accordance to Your Word, I declare and decree that I am fruitful, productive, and growing and that I am bearing fruit for Your kingdom. In Jesus' name I pray, Amen.*

SALVATION

This life-death concept is at the heart of salvation. It is solely through the death of Jesus that you and I have life. The Word is clear that just as death entered into the world through the sin of one man, so life came back and was restored through the death of another—namely, Jesus. (Romans 5:17-18)

In order to thrive in this new life more fully, we must learn to walk out this life-death concept on a daily basis. It is in learning to die to self that He can live through us more and more.

> *"I have been crucified with Christ; it is no longer I who live, but Christ lives in me."*
>
> *Galatians 2:20*

> *"He who loves his life will lose it, and he who hates his life in this world will keep it for eternal life."*
>
> John 12:24&25

The more you learn to die to your "self," the more fully you will live. This makes no sense in the natural world, but it resonates with my spirit! And though my soul wages war against this concept, it is by the spirit that I am able to come into this understanding of the life-death principle.

THE NEW PERSPECTIVE

When we come into an agreement with this life-death principle, we gain a new perspective and have a new understanding of our winters.

> *"I will open rivers in desolate heights, and fountains in the midst of the valleys; I will make the wilderness a pool of water, And the dry land springs of water. I will plant in the wilderness the cedar and the acacia tree, The myrtle and the oil tree; I will set in the desert the cypress tree and the pine, and the box tree together, That they may see and know, And consider and understand together, That the hand of the Lord has done this, And the Holy One of Israel has created it."*
>
> Isaiah 41:18-20

This passage reminds us that in the midst of winters, we can find life. More accurately, that God makes life come forth from death. And Isaiah tells us why: "That WE may see and know, and consider and understand that the hand of the Lord has done this" (emphasis mine). According to this passage, I should expect God to produce through what I perceive as dryness and desolation. That I should be watching for His hand in that manner. *The Message* paraphrases it like this...

> *"Everyone will see this. No one can miss it—unavoidable, indisputable, evidence that I, God, personally did this."*

I would like to propose that we too often give the devil credit

16

for what the Lord is doing and/or allowing in our lives. We give glory to the devil, while God is jumping up and down saying, "I want the entire world to know who I am and that I am working in every situation of your life, especially in the winters." God uses the devil and desires to turn every evil intention into our good and His glory.

> *"But as for you, you meant evil against me; but God meant it for good."*
> *Genesis 50:20a*

While God may not be the author of every circumstance, He is certainly still sovereign in the midst of it. His ear is never dull, His eye is never dim, nor is His arm too short. When we are confident in the knowledge of this truth, His glory will shine through and will shine abroad to those around us, even in our winters.

> *"Being confident of this very thing, that He who has begun a good work in you will complete it until the day of Jesus Christ."*
> *Philippians 1:6*

> *"Yea, though I walk through the valley of the shadow of death, I will fear no evil; For You are with me; Your rod and Your staff they comfort me."*
> *Psalm 23:4*

You can be confident when you choose to base your life on truths and not circumstances. And remember, if the Word of God says it, you can believe it!

It is not my circumstances that I stand upon, but rather the knowledge that God is with me and that He is using ALL things to refine me and shape me, in order that I would be complete in Him. This is good! And we can and should stand on this goodness. In fact we should expect goodness in all things!

> *"All things work together for good to those who love the Lord and are called according to His purpose."*
> *Romans 8:28*

The phrase "His purpose" means His design and His plan. The

Greek word actually denotes the idea of a deliberate plan. Our God is not an "eenie meenie miny mo" God! You will never hear God say, "Oops," or "What a surprise!" He is always a step ahead, leading the way with much intention and strategy.

PRAYER PRACTICE

God, I choose to be confident that You never leave me nor do You forsake me, but You are with me at all times. And not only are You with me, but You are working to bring me into who You have created me to be. I know, in accordance to Your Word, You are using all things to mature me and I agree that You are growing me daily even when I don't see You or feel You. I stand on your Word and in the authority You have given me, I declare that I am being transformed through my circumstances more into the image of Jesus Christ, from glory unto glory and that tonight when I go to bed, I will look a little more like Jesus. I declare and decree that all things in my life are good because I love You and I am called to work Your purpose. I agree that You are being deliberate and I rest in that. In the name of Jesus I pray, Amen.

Chapter 3 God-Driven Winters

et's take a look at times in the Bible that God Himself actually authored a season of winter for the purpose of refining and developing the heart of man. It is important that we see within the Word all that has been discussed so far.

> *"Therefore, behold, I will allure her, Will bring her into the wilderness, And speak comfort to her. I will give her her vineyards from there, And the Valley of Achor as a door of hope; She shall sing there, As in the days of her youth, As in the day when she came up from the land of Egypt. And it shall be, in that day," says the Lord, "That you will call Me 'My Husband,' And no longer call Me 'My Master.'"*
>
> *Hosea 2:14-17*

Recall I likened your winter season to that of a wilderness. A time when you are in a place of "nowhere" and experiencing a real dryness without direction. Look closely at this passage and see that God Himself is saying that He is "alluring" her into a wilderness. *To allure* means to *entice or persuade.* Why would God bring us into a place that the world and our flesh would consider miserable? That doesn't make sense to our human minds. In His infinite love, God may strip us down and isolate us in order to be alone with us and speak directly to us. He wants to intensify our intimacy and our reliance upon Him and Him alone. Read these verses paraphrased in *The Voice:*

> *"But once she has nothing, I'll be able to get through to her. I'll entice her and lead her out into the wilderness where we can be alone, and I'll speak right to her heart and try to win her back."*

Wow! What a beautiful description of what is going on. The

bigger picture of the heart of our situations and why God allows what He does.

LOVE THROUGH THE WINTER

God's desire is always to bring you into a greater understanding of His love for you and the depths of His passion. There is a shifting that He is forcing to come into play through this wilderness. A shift from looking at God as "Master" to "Husband." God is not content to have you view Him as a dictator or to be motivated in your work by fear of duty. He wants love to be your motive.

Compare it to a marriage. I love my husband and I know there are things in his life that are pleasing to him or make him feel loved. I desire to do those things for that purpose, because I desire for him to know and feel loved. He did not come with a handbook that stated all the things that I would need to do in order to keep him happy or for our marriage to be successful, but rather, I have learned through our relationship. It is the same with God. As you spend time with Him and pursue a relationship with Him, you learn of His heart, not of His rules.

I recently heard a sermon where the pastor described the verbiage on a sign that had been placed by a bed of flowers. The sign was written in three different languages. The first was is in German and read, "Picking flowers is prohibited." The second was in English and read, "Please don't pick the flowers." The third was in French and it read, "If you love the flowers, you won't pick them."

Through the three different languages, the message was the same. The difference is that the first conveyed the idea of obedience out of fear of authority. Prohibition promotes fear and intimidation. The second pulls on one's desire to be pleasing and "do the right thing." It feeds on your fear of what others would think and the desire to please people. But the third reminds the passer-by that if you love the flowers, then you won't pick them. It draws out the motive of love by reminding you that to pick the flowers would ultimately kill them.

And so it should be with the Lover of your Soul. Everything you do should be motivated by love, first and foremost. This requires falling in love with Him first. He sets you up to fall deeply into that place at times by alluring you into intimacy. Note that this passage says that the Valley of Achor, which means death, is a door of hope. Do you see the life-death principle here? You must recognize that it is the heart of the Father to produce greater life out of death.

POWER THROUGH THE WINTER

Even Jesus Himself was driven into the wilderness.

> *"Then Jesus, being filled with the Holy Spirit, returned from the Jordan and was led by the Spirit into the wilderness, being tempted for forty days by the devil. And in those days He ate nothing and afterward, when they had ended, He was hungry."*
>
> *Luke 4:1&2*

Jesus didn't just fall into the wilderness, but rather was led by the Spirit into that place. Again, we see that God often is the author of our winter seasons. In that season, He was tempted by the devil and was left feeling empty and parched. The passage goes on in Luke 4 to share all the ways the devil tempted Him, but I believe the key is found in verse 14.

> *"Then Jesus returned in the power of the Spirit to Galilee, and news of Him went out through all the surrounding region."*
>
> *Luke 4:17*

Note that when He went into the wilderness, He was filled with the Spirit, but when He came out, He was in the power of the Spirit. The Greek word used here for *filled* means to be "full, complete, lacking nothing, or perfect." But the word *power* comes from the Greek word *dynamis*, which means "strength power, and ability; power for performing miracles, moral power and excellence of soul." Do you see there was a purpose for His season of wilderness? There was a shift that took place through the trials and tribulations that He faced and that shift was to move Jesus from a place of a spiritual filling to demonstration of that filling. Through that wilderness Jesus became equipped for ministry. It was a

21

necessary wilderness and God was intentional in alluring Him into that place.

God's desire is the same for us. He often drives us into a winter season for the purpose of shifting us into the understanding of the power we have and can demonstrate. This equipping is imperative if we are going to accomplish the assignments He has for us on a daily basis. While in the winter, we too will face temptations and trials, but remember, God will never challenge us with what He has not equipped us to conquer.

> *"No temptation has overtaken you except such as is common to man; but God is faithful, who will not allow you to be tempted beyond what you are able, but with the temptation will also make the way of escape, that you may be able to bear it."*
>
> *1 Corinthians 10:13*

This verse does not say that God will not allow you to be tempted, but rather it says that He will always provide a way for you to stand in the midst of it. He uses trials and tribulations to draw His strength out of you; to force you to rely upon Him and step into your power as a believer in Christ. In the midst of your winters and as you face the harshness of the elements that comes with it, you can either cave, or you can rise up and take your rightful stand as more than a conqueror.

Do not focus on the trials, rather watch for what God is doing through the trials. Having an understanding that there is a *kairos* happening in the midst your linear trials will keep you expectant upon God and His heart. This is your hope! When your heart and mind are lined up with His and what He is doing, there is a lifting of your soul that doesn't come from the circumstances, but rather the knowledge of God and His love for you and in you.

> *"Now hope does not disappoint, because the love of God has been poured out in our hearts by the Holy Spirit who was given to us."*
>
> *Romans 5:5*

PROVEN THROUGH THE WINTER

Only God knows the fullness of your potential and all that you are made of. It is always His desire to bring you to the point of seeing you the way He sees you.

Isn't that how we look at our children? When we look at our infant, we don't see him or her stuck in the stage of crawling because we know that the child indeed has the DNA to walk, run and even dance... and we expect that it will happen. The same is true with how God sees us. We often feel like we are just infants... too small, too young, too weak and unable to see our ability to walk, run, or dance. God will drive us into a winter to show us or prove to us who we are. Often, people talk about whether or not God would actually test us, and I believe that Scripture is clear that He does. But it is not for His sake, rather it is for ours. In other words, He already knows what we've got; He just needs us to know what we've got.

Deuteronomy is a great book in which Moses is in a sense giving his final exhortation to the Israelites before his death. Mind you that they had spent forty years in the wilderness... stuck in a season of "winter." Forty years! That is a long time to wander around the desert waiting on God to deliver your promise. Deuteronomy is the "speech" Moses delivers at the pinnacle of their journey. In chapter 8, we learn of a purpose behind their time spent in the wilderness, which we can use to learn about our winter seasons.

> *"And you shall remember that the Lord your God led you all the way these forty years in the wilderness, to humble you and test you, to know what was in your heart, whether you would keep His commandments or not. So He humbled you, allowed you to hunger, and fed you with manna which you did not know nor did your fathers know, that He might make you know that man shall not live by bread alone; but man lives by every word that proceeds from the mouth of the Lord."*
>
> *Deuteronomy 8:2&3*

God led them in the wilderness for the purpose of exposing their hearts and their potential.

PUSHING OUR LIMITS

Let's go back and read these verses as presented in *The Message.*

> *"Remember every road that God led you on for those forty years in the wilderness, pushing you to your limits, testing you so that he would know what you were made of..."*

God will indeed push us to our limits, and that is good. Listen, we need to know our full potential and the strength that we possess through the Holy Spirit, and the only way we will come to know the depths of that strength is through our winters. Body builders measure their strength through the amount of weight they can bear. The amount of weight *proves* their strength. Furthermore, they increase their strength by increasing weight. The more weight that is added, or the more resistance, the more their strength grows! Who knows the potential of how much physical strength I might have? I have never trained extensively through weight lifting, but if I did, I am willing to bet that I would be surprised at the strength that would manifest in my body. So it is with our spirits. The weight of our circumstances *will* strengthen us if we allow it to, thus proving the depths of our abilities to bear up under the heaviness of everything in life that threatens and weighs us down.

> *"In this you greatly rejoice, though now for a little while, if need be, you have been grieved, by various trials, that the genuineness of your faith, being much more precious than gold that perishes, though it is tested by fire, may be found to praise and glory at the revelation of Jesus Christ."*
>
> 1 Peter 1:6&7

"To be found" means "to be discovered or to be proven." It is good to discover the depths of your own faith and to have your faith proven... not necessarily to others, but to yourself!

WHAT IS IT?

One of the things I want to point out in the Deuteronomy passage is that God fed the Israelites with manna every day. The

24

word *manna* actually means "What is it?" Think about this with me for a moment. The Israelites were wandering about in the wilderness with no visual of where they were going and no clue when they would get there. And all the while, they were fed a daily dose of "What is it?" Boy, can I relate! Being in a season where every day, more and more unknowns are dropped out of nowhere and you find yourself saying, "What is this?" One thing after another: "What is this? I don't even know what to call this or how to define what is happening!" Imagine the Israelites saying every day, "What is this?" It's kind of comical if you think about it. I love that we serve a God with a sense of humor! But ultimately, we can connect with trudging through a season of unknowns and indefinable happenings where we find ourselves saying, "What in the world is this?"

But why? Why did God give them manna?

> *"...that He might make you know that man shall not live by bread alone; but man lives by every word that proceeds from the mouth of the Lord."*

Why does God allow so much "What is this?" in our lives? Why does He often feed us daily doses of unknowns? God is refining our ability to live, not in accordance to what you have or don't have, or what you see or don't see, or what is happening or not happening, but rather what He says. We are not to live according to the dose of the world or our circumstances, but the Word of God! We have to hold to what we know God has said to us and His promises. That is solely what got me through a recent winter that I walked through.

❧ PRAYER PRACTICE

> *God, there are so many things in my life that are unknown to me. I feel like I am losing any sense of control in my winter. But I know that it is by Your Word that I am sustained and that by Your Word I am satisfied. I receive Your Word as truth and I eat of it. I am filled with energy and tenacity to press in*

and press on by the power of Your Word. I thank You that when all else fails, Your Word perseveres. I declare and decree that I agree and am content with Your promises and that I am at peace despite my circumstances. For Your Word IS my light and WILL illuminate my path and I trust You. In the sweet name of Jesus I pray, Amen.

MY RECENT WINTER

This past year, Crazy8 Ministries was faced with the challenge of needing to find new land. We were under a time crunch and had many obstacles that needed to be overcome in order for us to move to the next level. So, on faith, I started a huge land campaign and invited the entire community to be a part of it. I blasted out on social media what we were doing and my confidence in God to come through in a miraculous way. We needed to raise money, we needed to find land, we needed to get approved for a loan, and we needed to pick up an entire ministry and move; all while still housing and taking care of women and children. I had the weight of the responsibility of making sure this all happened in a timely manner. I knew the "unknowns" could overwhelm me, but I chose to focus on the Word of God. I fed myself on it, and it is what got me through.

If that wasn't enough going on, in the middle of this campaign, I was facing several personal challenges within our family and the struggles that some of my children were walking through. And the challenges were not with my "littles" who were living in our home, but with my college kids who were far away from us. This was something I had never faced before... mothering from a distance and truly trusting the Lord to walk with your kids. How many of you ladies know that as women, we can rise up under many trials and challenges in our lives, but when it comes to our kiddos, we are easily fainthearted? I can honestly say it was by far one of the most difficult seasons I have ever walked through. There was so much going on at one time. Much of it I could not share with even my closest staff. So, there were practical things that were taking place that made me feel like I was hidden, because I couldn't share and connect with anyone in regard to how I was feeling. And in the midst of all this, I had the weight of the responsibility of trying to find the perfect property. Every time I thought I had found the perfect land, it ended up not being the right one. I began to doubt whether or not I even could hear from God anymore. I thought, "I am missing the mark every time I shoot an arrow, I am off!" That doubt began to creep into every aspect of my life and I struggled deeply with losing my confidence in my ability to lead this ministry.

In the middle of this, people would come up to me and say, "Lisa, you just need to have faith." Listen, I am going to be very real with you when I say, please do <u>not</u> say that to someone who is walking through a winter season because it insinuates that person doesn't have faith. In a season when you are clinging to anything you can to find strength and encouragement, this statement is not helpful or uplifting. It only points to your lack or "what isn't" and how you are "falling short" and need to be "doing better."

There were nights that I spent crying out to the Lord while people were freely giving me their opinion and telling me what I "needed to do." Plans were being changed and things were being redirected on a daily basis and I was losing faith in my own ability to even hear from Him. I am just keeping it real here and sharing what this season was like for me. And, keep in mind that "all the world" was watching me and the progress of Crazy8 during all of this because God had called me to put this campaign out for the community to follow so that everyone could see what God was doing. All I kept thinking was, "All they are seeing is how much I keep missing the mark." It stunk! It was like I was living Psalm 6:6 that says, "I was weary with my groaning; every night I soak my bed with tears..." And though there were people that were alongside of me through this winter, honestly, there was nobody that understood what I was going through. No one.

It was only in clinging to the Word and what I knew He had promised that I found strength to get up every day and look for land and seek funding and make connections and coordinate fundraisers and press on toward the goal. Sometimes we just need to choose to get on with it! Remember and be confident in all God has spoken to you and live accordingly! That is what got me through, and it is what stirs you up and makes you tenacious. The Word of God and my confidence in it is what made me come to a place where I wouldn't take no for an answer.

Remember, it is not about the little details that come to distract us or pose to steal our peace. The little foxes will always come and try to steal the fullness of your time in the vineyard. (Song of Songs 2:5) It is by staying focused on what God is doing and your understanding of His purpose of the season that you are able to master it!

⌒ PRAYER PRACTICE

> *Father, I rebuke the devil in my life and his attempt to steal, kill, and destroy my walk with you. I refuse to pay attention to him and his antics, but I am wholly focused upon You and Your love. I am saturated by Your Presence and my eye is upon You. For You are the Author and Perfector of my faith and I know that You are working to deepen my life so that my vineyard will bear more fruit. In Jesus' name I pray, Amen.*

It was during that season, every day when I woke up, that the Lord reminded me of Abraham who said, "I will sacrifice anything, I will do anything you tell me to do...even my life, I would give up for you." And, God called him on the carpet and said, "I want you to sacrifice Isaac."

Scripture doesn't say, but I would imagine that with every step Abraham took, he had to seriously consider, "Will I take the next step? Will I still trust God? Will I still believe Him? Even though You, God, have told me that my promise is in this one thing You are now calling me to lay at the altar?" Similarly, I wrestled saying, "This doesn't make any sense God! This is a ministry that YOU have placed in my heart. This is a ministry that YOU started and I didn't ask for it." But, with every step, I heard the Lord saying, "Would you sacrifice everything?" And with every step, I had to "re-decide." I just did... every step! In the end, my faith was proven. Not because land came through in a miraculous way, but because I was refined and fell more in love with the Lord in a visible way and the Lord ultimately was glorified through it all.

I am here to tell you that it was one of the best seasons that I

28

have ever walked through because my faith was proven. Not to you, and not to God, but to me!

I can honestly say now that everything that I said that I stand for, now I KNOW I stand for it. All because God afforded me a time of winter where I could stand and conquer in the midst of the harsh elements of the circumstances. What I always said I believed became a reality. Job had the same revelation.

"I have heard of You by the hearing of the ear, But now my eye sees You."

Job 42:5

This season was filled with learning new things in regard to business and spending much of my time doing things that did not come easy for me. And, in the middle of it, I seemed to be failing all over the place. What I held on to was the vision and passion that God had placed inside of me for a greater ministry that served more people. I kept saying, "God, I didn't ask for this...You asked me. And, for what it's worth, I am still here and I am still available. I don't have much, but what I DO have, I am bringing to You and I am trusting you to work the rest out!" And, He did, in an incredible way! But what He was doing was more than just what we saw in the natural or through our *chronos* events. He was working things out spiritually in me and in others around me. Now, people ask, "How did this happen? How did you end up with such an incredible piece of property?" And my answer is, "I don't know, but I know that God blesses us when we are faithful." You see, even though I can't answer what happened circumstantially, what I CAN say is that now I am more confident in the heart of God than ever before.

Mastering your winter involves watching for how He is deepening your love and intimacy, how He is equipping you for your assignments with His power and authority, and how He is desiring to prove to you who you are and that you've got what it takes. Expect God to work for your good and watch for it! That perspective will have you heading into your winters with a new attitude and a new confidence that will make you tenacious for your victory!

Chapter 4 The Dangers of Your Winter

here are things that we should be aware of that will pose to trip us up in our winter seasons. These are the things that we will get sucked into that will keep us from our mastery of winter. By exposing these things, we can gird up and be prepared ahead of time. This is part of what it means to put the armor of God on BEFORE you go into battle.

> *"...Put on the whole armor of God, that you may be able to stand against the wiles of the devil... Therefore take up the whole armor of God, that you may be able to withstand in the evil day, and having done all, to stand."*
>
> *Ephesians 6:11&13*

We can learn through Scripture the ways our flesh is prone to fall and through that gain an understanding of how we can be preventatively proactive. This is what putting on the armor of God looks like. Being armed with the Word and practicing the Word so that I am schooled and automatic. If I can't practice truths during the easy seasons, how in the world can I practice them during the harsh ones? Let's consider the dangers of winter and be ready and armed with the Word.

THE DANGER OF FEELINGS OF ABANDONMENT AND ISOLATION

The enemy will want you to feel alone and abandoned in your winter season, but you know those feelings are not true. How do you know it? Because the Word says so, and remember, if the Word says it, I believe it!

> *"For He Himself has said, "I will never leave you nor forsake you. So that we may boldly say: "The Lord is my helper; I will*

31

not fear. What can man do to me?"

Hebrews 13:5&6

God has declared to us the promise of His presence at all times. Why? So that we will know Him, boldly, as our Helper. He wants you to be confident in His presence and by standing on this knowledge you can ward off the fear of being alone. You must agree with this truth at all times, especially in seasons of winter. Practicing the presence of God at all times is how you gird up and prepare. Being aware of God in your everyday life and acknowledging His hand in all things is a great place to start. Don't talk about God as if He is not in the room with you, but rather acknowledge His presence. This is how you armor up and train towards knowing His presence, even when you don't see it or feel it. Psalm 121 is a great passage to memorize and declare on a regular basis.

PRAYER PRACTICE

Where does my help come from? Lord, I know my help comes from You and You alone. I lift my eyes to You and I look to You. I speak with confidence that You will not allow my foot to slip. It is not by my strength, but by Your grace that I stand. I thank You that You never fall asleep on me and that You are alert to my needs. I am aware of Your eye upon me and Your presence that is ever with me and keeping me in the way of everlasting. I praise You for preserving me no matter where I go and in this day I will speak of Your presence in all that I do! In the name of Jesus I pray, Amen.

Declare these words daily and you will come into the fullness of the truth of them. The Word becomes fleshed out in us and we are able to boldly declare His presence and rest in peace even when our circumstances scream that we are abandoned and our feelings verify this lie through emotions of loneliness.

"And the Lord went before them by day in a pillar of cloud to lead the way and by night in a pillar of fire to give them light, so as to go by day and night. He did not take away the pillar of cloud by day or the pillar of fire by night from before the people."

Exodus 13:21&22

We read here the truth of His presence to the Israelites during their time in the wilderness. He was always with them. So when, not if, but when we feel alone, when we feel isolated, we can stand on what we learn about God in His Word and what we know is true and not on what we feel or are experiencing. Are there times in our lives when we are genuinely, circumstantially in the natural alone? Absolutely! But we are not to live according to the natural, but rather according to the Spirit.

☙ PRAYER PRACTICE

For I am first and foremost a spirit being who has a soul that dwells in a body. I know this full well and I declare and decree that I am living based on the truth of my spirit and I command my soul to sit down and line up with the excellence of the Spirit of the living God who lives and breathes within me! For though I feel alone and am genuinely alone in my circumstance, I know that Thou art with me in my valley and You comfort me in this place. I receive Your presence and Your love right now. That is my truth! In the name of Jesus I pray, Amen.

Walking in His presence doesn't mean that you won't ever experience times of being alone or times of isolation. I do not dismiss the fact that sometimes you really are alone in how you feel in your soul. I counsel women all the time who have been abandoned by their husbands, after being abandoned by their fathers. I validate their season and I validate their feeling, but I am here to tell you that there is a greater truth to stand on and that you do not have to be a victim of loneliness. You can rise above the circumstance and say, "Though the world has forsaken me, though my husband has left me, though my father dismissed me, MY GOD has never left me nor has He forsaken me. For He has written my name upon the palms of His hands and I agree!" (Psalm 27:10, Isaiah 49:16)

One of the enemy's greatest deceptions is to isolate you and make you feel alone and abandoned. He will twist the truth of your circumstances to deceive you. He wants you to choose isolation because he knows there is strength "in the pack." Think about how animals work in the animal kingdom. When a lion is running after a pack, he will always try and veer one off and pull it away from the pack. Once he accomplishes that, the prey is weak and loses the power of the pack. Then, the lion devours it. But let me say this, being alone is more than just a physical state. It is possible for me to be in a room full of people, yet feel completely alone... like no one sees me, or acknowledges me, or understands me. Loneliness is a state of mind, which is great news! It means that we can choose not to feel lonely, whether it is perceived or real.

You see, walking in His presence means declaring what is true and forcing your soul to line up with what you know the Word says. James 1:21 reminds us that it is through the implantation of the Word that the soul is rescued and saved. Trust me, my soul often desperately needs rescued! The point is, it is not the absence of isolation or lonely circumstances, but rather the knowledge that you choose the company of the Lord despite that isolation and loneliness.

I recall a season in my life during which my husband was working two jobs and going to school. Although my home was filled with the sound and presence of four children, I felt very alone. In one sense, I was because my husband was not home much, but in another sense I wasn't because I homeschooled, so my kids were home all day. Nonetheless, I struggled with a deep sense of loneliness. I recall being very intentional to seek the Lord as "My Company." Sounds crazy, I know, but God says that He is the great, "I Am," meaning, "I am whatever and whoever you need me to be." So even though there was a very real chronological, linear season that I was experiencing, I learned to look for God and expect God to be working in the midst of it. I began to practice His presence and found that after many weeks, my loneliness began to dissipate. My circumstances didn't change, but my perspective did. I began to focus on the season spiritually and noted that God was working in the spirit realm through the natural to deepen me and intensify my intimacy with Him. I came to know Him in the ordinary and mundane things in the life of a stay-at-home mom. I learned that God was very interested in the daily operations of my life, such as laundry, housekeeping, grocery shopping, cooking, schooling, etc. I would not change that season for anything!

HIS PRESENCE

I want to side-step for a moment here and point out the importance of teaching and training others to rely upon the presence of the Lord and not on our presence. As a friend or a mentor, we do a disservice to let our friends or disciples rely upon us as their "fix" to loneliness. Often, especially for women, we want to be a martyr and we have a "need to be needed." If I am completely honest, I enjoy being needed. It makes me feel useful. I am in no way downplaying the importance of the ministry of presence. I am blessed with a couple of people on my staff that can simply walk into my office and a peace comes flooding through the room and into my soul. It is a sweet gift that God has given to them, I think specifically for me. However, I am not lost or lonely without them. I have seen people form what are called "ungodly soul ties" with others. This is a form of idolatry because you rely upon that person instead of upon God. God does use people in your life to encourage and lift you up, but the goal is to direct you toward Him and not toward the person doing the encouraging. By teaching someone to run to Him, we are equipping instead of enabling.

> *"For we do not have a High Priest who cannot sympathize with our weaknesses, but was in all points tempted as we are, yet without sin. Let us therefore come boldly to the throne of grace, that we may obtain mercy and find grace to help in time of need."*
>
> *Hebrews 4:15&16*

Have you ever desperately wanted someone to know exactly

how you're feeling? Have you ever yourself wanted to be able to discern your own feelings? This verse is such a beautiful promise that God Himself is familiar with all of our challenges and all that we are encountering. He is not unable to sympathize. That word in the Greek means "to be affected with the same feeling as another." This is something that as a human, I cannot do. I can at best empathize with someone, and sometimes, I can relate if I have walked through what they are walking through. Because I am not God, I cannot connect the way He can and actually feel or be affected by their hurts or challenges like Him. The King James Version says it like this:

> *"For we have not a high priest which cannot be touched with the feeling of our infirmities..."*

Consider Isaiah 53:12, which reads:

> *"And He was numbered with the transgressors, And He bore the sin of many, And made intercession for the transgressors."*

This is another truth reminding that Jesus Himself not only can relate, but He bore our infirmities. This is why He is so acquainted with all of our challenges. Knowing this truth, you can be bold in approaching Him. You are not going to shock Him with your thoughts and emotions, nor is He repulsed by your behavior. He does not grow weary of your whining nor does He dismiss your groanings. I don't know about you, but I can't do what He does for people, and unfortunately, I often don't have the same patience and compassion that He has. This is why it is important to take others by the hand and usher them into His presence instead of just ours.

I have learned to spend more time praying with people. By doing this, I am taking them by the hand to the throne room, stirring up His presence by praise and then letting His presence work. He is sufficient! Too often we rely upon the presence and words of man, which can work in the soul, and temporarily make us feel better. But the transformation that we need to be changed permanently only happens by the Spirit of the Lord. Remember, loneliness is not about our external circumstances, it runs deep out of the heart of a man.

"Deep calls unto deep at the noise of Your waterfalls; All Your waves and billows have gone over me."

Psalm 42:7

The waves of His presence wash over our souls to adjust things deep within us! We have the power to touch lives, but only God has the power to transform them. This transformation causes a shift in thinking that screams, "Though my circumstances haven't changed, I have!"

℮ PRAYER PRACTICE

Father, Your presence is like the waves of the sea that overwhelms me and consumes me. Just like being in the depths, so Your love surrounds me even when I don't feel it or see it. I praise You for Your promise and I declare that the depths of You are calling and pursuing the depths of me. I receive Your call and I walk in the fullness of what I know to be true. Thank You for by-passing my soul and speaking directly into my spirit and transforming me from the inside out. I declare that today I will walk in the confidence of Your company in my life. In Jesus' name I pray, Amen.

THE DANGER OF COMPLACENCY

There is a difference between contentment and complacency. Although we should be content in our winter, we should never be complacent there. God desires to move you beyond winter and you should be expectant and ready to move.

"Whether it was two days, a month or a year that the cloud remained above the tabernacle, the children of Israel would remain encamped and not journey; but when it was taken up, they would journey. At the command of the Lord they remained encamped, and at the command of the Lord they journeyed; they kept the charge of the lord, at the command of the Lord by the hand of Moses."

Numbers 9:22&23

37

The Israelites were ready to go! The minute the cloud would move, they moved, but if it stayed, they stayed. They were content to wait on the Lord, but they were not complacent. They were not lazy or apathetic or unwilling to move. In fact, they were expecting movement. So we should be in our winters. We must accept where we are, but trust God for where we are not. Sadly, we often get complacent and settle in, calling it "being content," and we no longer expect advancement from God.

SEEKING VS. EXPECTING

There is a difference between seeking and expecting. One is looking for God, but the other is watching with a hopeful confidence that He will respond and move on your behalf. To expect means "to anticipate or regard as likely to happen." This is a bold mindset that religion or the world will often call arrogant.

> *"My voice You shall hear in the morning, O Lord; In the mornings I will direct it to You. And I will look up."*
> *Psalm 5:3*

The verse in the New International Version reads: "In the morning I lay my request before you and wait expectantly." In Greek, the phrase *to look* denotes the idea of "arranging, anticipating, preparing and putting in order." The psalmist is not just seeking the Lord, he is expecting that God will hear and will respond to the point that he is getting things ready and in order. This is how the children of Israel were. They were ready to move. They girded up and were on the lookout. They expected that they would move on toward the Promised Land.

MY EXPECTATIONS

When I understand the Kingdom principles that I learn through His Word, I can boldly expect that there is fruit in my winter. I can expect that He is growing me, I can expect that He is working things out for my good and His glory, I can expect that He is maturing and completing me, I can expect that His presence will be all around me, I can expect that whether I am in season or out of season, that I will bear fruit and there is productivity in my life. I expect that people are going to come around me and they are going to taste and see that the Lord is good! I expect that people are going to be healed, saved and delivered, I expect that people are going to be changed in the presence of the Lord, and I expect transformation in their lives. I expect more than just a touch from God. I expect that He is imparting a lifestyle into me! I expect the supernatural, I expect big things, I expect signs, I expect miracles, and I expect wonders of the Lord. He is a supernatural God and I expect Him to show up and be who He is! I am no longer shy about placing an expectation upon God. His Spirit and Word prompt me to anticipate the fullness of who He is and how He works. I expected God to show up and bring us land, and He did! I am not saying that I never waver or that I don't struggle with doubt, I already shared that I do, but at the end of every day I expect Him still to be God. A supernatural God. I am resolved and resolute in who I know Him to be and I expect Him to show up in every situation and move. I am determined, and though there may be times of wavering, I will not be moved!

Part of our problem is we place no expectations on God. At best, we expect Him to show up like a human and not like God. And, if He doesn't show up, we wonder why! We must draw on His heart, rely on His character, and force the natural to comply with the supernatural hand of God. We say we believe it, in fact, you are likely nodding as your read this, yet we don't stand on it boldly and expect it in our own lives. Having expectations is one of the best ways to ward off complacency because it keeps you looking forward with a hopeful anticipation. God is always moving us and growing us. In nature this is a fact, so why would we expect anything less? Don't settle!

℮ PRAYER PRACTICE

> *Father, I know what Your Word says about You and who You are and the way You work. You are a supernatural God and I look to You and expect you to work in supernatural ways. I expect that in my life, You will do things that cannot be explained and will point to You and Your presence working in and*

through me. I thank You for all You have done and I seek Your forgiveness for not pulling on Your arm for even more. I step into the boldness that You give me and with an assurance of faith I seek You for things that are unexplainable in the natural. In Jesus' name I pray, Amen.

THE DANGER OF DISCONTENTMENT

Being discontent and becoming a whiner and complainer is a danger in the winter. Suddenly, the glass is always half empty instead of half full, and all you can think about is what you don't have instead of what you do. You have the power to choose.

> *"I call heaven and earth as witnesses today against you, that I have set before you life and death, blessing and cursing; therefore choose life, that both you and your descendants may live."*
>
> *Deuteronomy 30:19*

This is a powerful verse in that God reminds that we have the power to choose for ourselves the path we want to take. Now remember, I am talking about perspective and our attitude. You must choose thoughts that are filled with life and goodness. Being content means you refuse to be dismayed or disheartened. Instead, you are tenacious for joy.

☙ PRAYER PRACTICE

Lord, You have given me the power to choose and the wisdom to choose wisely. Your Word says that I have the mind of Christ. I declare and decree that I think like You and I choose like You. Every thought that I have is in line with the way that You think and every choice that I make is one of life and blessings. I set my mind upon Your heart and Your Word and I look forward to the fruit of being sound minded and making wise choices in this day! In the name of Jesus I pray, Amen.

When I meet with clients, especially those who are in a season of depression, the tendency is for them to focus on all the things in their lives that are wrong or all that their life is missing, or all the ways their life is falling short. They talk about their depletion or the lack in their lives. In other words, what they don't have or all that is "wrong." We could spend the entire hour talking about all the things wrong and never get to what is right. I must focus on shifting them from problems to solution. I have had so many clients come to me who have seen counselors their whole lives. They are therefore very good at identifying all their issues and even the reasons for their issues. Unfortunately, they often are unable to know how to fix their issues or move beyond them. I guess they feel being able to identify and justify is enough. Not for me, I want to sanctify and be completely healed.

It's easy to focus on the negative, however the Bible commands us to set our minds on the positive.

> "Finally, brethren, whatever things are true, whatever things are noble, whatever things are just, whatever things are pure, whatever things are lovely, whatever things are of good report, if there is any virtue and if there is anything praiseworthy—meditate on these things."
>
> *Philippians 4:8*

The word *meditate* means to "count, compute, calculate, reckon inward, or take into account." It is the idea of taking inventory. We all know how to meditate. When you are worrying, you are meditating on your fear. When you are whining or complaining, you are meditating on your unhappiness. Wherever you choose to let your mind reside will control your emotions. Focusing on lack will breed discontent.

While doing our land campaign, I noticed when I focused on the amount that we needed, I began to speak a lot about "how much more we needed," or "how short we were of our goal." The Lord spoke to me through two passages to correct my thinking.

First, He spoke through the story of the feeding of the multitudes. He reminded me that the disciples' complaint or concern was: "We *only* have two fish and five loaves." But Jesus didn't focus on lack. Instead He told them to start with what they had on faith, and then watch Him multiply. Jesus forced them to function on faith and draw out the supernatural work of the Father. His encouragement was, in a sense, "Look at what I have provided for you!" Jesus wasn't concerned about the lack, He focused on what was instead of what was not. He focused on what He had, instead of what He did not have.

Second, God showed me the same concept through the story of Elisha and the widow in 2 Kings 4. A widow came to Elisha in deep distress and *cried out*, meaning, "to moan or weep uncontrollably." And she began to tell him all the problems she was encountering. These were legitimate problems. "Here is all that I don't have. My husband has died and I don't have money and I can't pay my bills, and I am about to also lose my sons and my freedom." (2 Kings 4:1) In verse 2, Elisha responded, "Tell me, what do you have in the house?" Do you see what he did? He shifted her focus and her complaint from her lack to her provision. He asked, "What DO you have?" He went on to challenge her to use what she did have and start with that on faith. Her faith forced the miracle or provision to manifest. Same message!

God said to me that I needed to stop focusing on what we didn't have and start moving on what we did have. This required faith, but remember the disciples with the multitude? I can imagine that they looked at the two fish and five loaves and then looked at the multitude and must have thought, "Really? Two plus five does not equal five thousand!" But, as they started feeding, the provision multiplied. You see, two plus five plus God equals more than enough. I think my favorite part of that miracle is that there were basketfuls left over! That is our God—a God of overflow. Faith had to come first, and the miracle followed. Their faith spurred on the miracle.

"And these signs will follow those who believe."
Mark 16:17

Discontentment is a restless desire or craving for something that one does not have or that is missing. The devil will breed that discontent by tempting you to focus on your lack! This is why you must shift to what is instead of what is not.

Listen to what happens to the Israelites in their

discontentment.

> *"We remember the fish which we ate freely in Egypt, the cucumbers, the melons, the leeks, the onions, and the garlic; but now our whole being is dried up; there is nothing at all except this manna before our eyes!"*
>
> *Numbers 11:5&6*

Their whining and complaining dried up their being. There is nothing worse than a dry and depleted soul. The world, the devil, and our flesh will suck the life out of our souls and will leave us feeling puny and faint, dried up and shriveled. This is the path we choose when we do not heed the words of Philippians 4:8 and choose our own murmuring instead.

Paul learned how to prevent this feeling of weakness and dryness and shares his secret with us.

> *"Not that I speak in regard to need, for I have learned in whatever state I am to be content; I know how to be abased, and I know how to abound. Everywhere and in all things I have learned both to be full and to be hungry, both to abound and to suffer need. I can do all things through Christ who strengthens me."*
>
> *Philippians 4:11-13*

Look at the very first thing he says, "Not that I speak in regard to need..." meaning, "I don't speak about the things that I need." The Message says it like this, "Actually, I don't have a sense of needing anything personally." The word *regard* means "attention or concern for something, esteem or significant look." He is reiterating that he pays no attention to what is not or what he is lacking. He does not esteem or elevate his need, or make it the object of his attention. That is powerful! When we focus only on the last part of the verse that says, "I can do all things through Christ who strengthens me," but we don't highlight what brings him to that understanding and resounding declaration, then we miss out. By not regarding our need, we learn to be content. Paul is clear that he has in no way arrived, but that he too is in the process of learning to walk in contentment. He states here that with the right perspective, he can be in a state of hunger, but still be full. Yes, you can be in the famine of winter, yet still feast on the goodness of God, you can be in a drought, but still experience the Living Water.

PRAYER PRACTICE

> *God, I shift my thoughts onto that which I have and You have given. For You have done great things and I set my mind upon those things. I recall all that You are and You have never, not once, let me down or forsaken me. You are the same yesterday, today and forever, and I therefore count on you to continue to be thus for me. I set my heart to praise, I loose my lips to thanks, and release my feet to dance solely because You are good. I thank you that in my yucky circumstance, I find fullness and fruit. I am satisfied in You and I am content. You are my Shepherd and I shall not want! In Jesus' name I pray, Amen.*

Paul is also clear that his strength comes from Christ alone. Think about all the circumstances, places, and people that you try to draw strength from. Let's reverse it. Think about all the circumstances, places, and people who suck the life out of you. When you can answer those thoughts, you have found sources of idols in your life. It is not people, places, or circumstances that should strengthen us, nor should we allow them to weaken us. But rather Christ alone is my source of strength. I am in no way saying that God does not use these other things to encourage us and build us up, but the foundation of my strength should come from God and His love… that's it! Everything else is the cherry on top!

The word *contentment* in Philippians 3 denotes the idea of being "independent of external circumstances." Our contentment doesn't come from our circumstances. There should be no connection. Contentment has nothing to do with our happenings, but when we think it does, we end up waiting until our circumstances bring it about. They never will!

When my kids were little and I was struggling with clinical depression, I continually said things like, "When the baby sleeps

44

through the night..." or "When the kids are older..." or "When the weather is warmer..." or "When I have more time..." or "When we have more money..." You see, I was waiting on my life and my season to be "just right" before I chose to be content. Guess what? You will wait forever because contentment is independent of your external circumstances. It comes from the knowledge of a spiritual work happening in all that you see in the natural. It comes from inside of me, not from the things happening around me! It is in escaping the natural and stepping into the throne room regularly to be saturated by His love that contentment just happens and becomes who I am.

WHO'S TO BLAME?

Often, we get stuck in the blame game. We blame people and ourselves for our circumstances or our lack. The Israelites did this in their wilderness; a prime example of our inclination as humans.

"And in the morning you shall see the glory of the Lord for He hears your complaints against Him. But what are we that you complain against us? For the Lord hears your complaints which you make against Him. And what are we? Our complaints are not against us but against the Lord."
Exodus 16:7&8

Moses is clear that their bone to pick was not with him, but with God. He pointed out to them that their fussiness was not an offense to him, it was against God. To blame people is to give them credit for all that is going on in your life and it negates the sovereignty of God. Just because people play a part in your life does not make their role in your life more powerful than God's. In fact, the only power people have is the power you choose to give them.

The Israelites dismissed the will of God and how He was working and why He allowed their wilderness. They were so focused on their lack that they missed out on God and what He was doing for them and in them. They were discontent and unhappy where the Lord had them and were unable to recognize that their wrestling was not with man, but with God.

It is easy for us to blame our friends, it is easy for us to blame our spouses, it is easy for us to blame our kids, our bosses, our circumstances, our finances, etc. The reality is if you are walking in discontent and whining and complaining, and frankly, being a drain to everyone around you, your complaint is actually against God. When I was looking for land and under a "time crunch," the inclination was to blame people for the situation. I battled even the perceptions that people wanted to believe and stir up for why we were under such a time crunch. But I was very aware that the Lord Himself brought us to that place and that He was in control. To complain would have been against Him and Him alone. If you have a complaint, that's OK, but take it to the throne room and reason it out with the Lord. That does not bother Him.

"'Come now, Let us reason together,' says the Lord..."
Isaiah 1:18

God actually invites us to reason and contend with Him about the things we are fussy about. This is what the whole book of Job is about. Job reasons with the Lord in regard to his season of winter. We lose perspective when we blame everyone and everything else for our circumstances and we miss out on what God is doing in our own lives.

If I am truly saturated and in agreement with the love of God, none of these other things will matter. I will not be rejected, I will not have fear, I will have no anxiety, I will have no offense and I will not be fussing or discontent because His love covers all of those things!

In Hebrew, the word *complain* or *murmur* also denotes the idea of "lodging or stopping." In other words, it is like saying, "I am stuck here in this spot, I am lodged in this place because I have chosen to dwell on my 'have nots' and all the things that I don't like about my life right now." There is no moving beyond your circumstances when you choose to engage in complaining. Complaining is being enslaved to your problems. You are literally allowing yourself to be taken captive by them. Those problems will quickly take over your mind and your emotions. Again, recall that we are to focus on what is excellent and praiseworthy. (Phil. 4:8) Did you know that *to praise* means to "repetitively talk about or exalt" something? This is what we do when we complain. Our problem becomes the object of our praise. This will keep you stuck or lodged in your problem! It is a terrible place to be, and this kind of person is terrible to hang around. God teaches us and trains us through His Word how to walk in contentment. Instead, we often prefer to say, "I hear You God and what You are telling me, but I would like to stop here for a while and abide in my problems." Come on now, let's be honest! You know what you need to do, now do it! This is what sets apart those who have knowledge of victory from those who are walking in it.

THE DANGER OF WEARINESS AND FAINTHEARTEDNESS

"And let us not grow weary of doing good, for in due season we will reap, if we do not give up."

Galatians 6:9

The word *weary* here means to be "utterly spiritless, to be worn out, to be exhausted."

In 1 Samuel 30, David and his mighty men have, in confidence and victory, totally wiped out Ziklag. They came back to a horrible surprise. All of their women and children were taken captive while they were gone. They came back, hoping for celebration, but instead they experience devastation. Not exactly what they were expecting or prepared for. The Bible says that they began to weep, and all of David's mighty warriors, his friends, and his supporters wanted to stone him. Those friends that supported him when he was succeeding now turned against him and blamed him for their loss. At a time when David likely needed the most support and the most encouragement, those whom he battled with, slept with, and bathed with became his enemies.

"Then David and the people who were with him lifted up their voices and wept, until they had no more power to weep."

1 Samuel 30:4

Listen, that is weariness. That is faintheartedness. When you weep until all your strength is gone and you can't even cry anymore. I am not sure if you have ever experienced that level of weariness, but it can draw the life from your physical body. The

Word says they were *greatly distressed* and *all the people grieved.*
See what David did in the midst of this devastating season he had
just been thrown into.

> *"David was greatly distressed because the men were talking*
> *of stoning him; each one was bitter in spirit because of his*
> *sons and daughters.* **But David found strength in the LORD**
> **his God.** "
>
> 1 Samuel 30:6
> (emphasis mine)

David strengthened himself in the Lord. He had no friends he
could turn to, he couldn't even turn to his wife for encouragement
since she had been taken captive. David was already hated by King
Saul and his army who were continuously trying to kill him. Even
so, David turned to the Lord and he strengthened himself IN THE
LORD. It says that he asked for the ephod to be brought to him so
that he could inquire directly from the Lord. Some versions say he
encouraged himself in the Lord. The Hebrew word denotes "to
strengthen, to prevail, to harden, to be firm, to be resolute, or to
grow firm; to withstand, to hold strongly, to support, or to repair."
This expands the fullness of what God can do for us, and more
importantly what He wants to do for you in the seasons that pose to
make you weary and fainthearted.

> *"So David inquired of the Lord saying, 'Shall I pursue this*
> *troop? Shall I overtake them?' And He answered him, 'Pursue,*
> *for you shall surely overtake them and without fail recover*
> *all.'"*
>
> 1 Samuel 30:8

Look at the response he gets from God. God Himself brings a
resounding assurance directly to David's heart telling him that he
"shall surely overtake them and without fail recover all." Is this not
what our heart needs in our seasons of lack and loss and
devastation? In our winters, do we not desperately need that still,
small voice that whispers in our ears that we shall recover ALL?
There is no one else who can promise you that. People might say it,
or they might give you advice on how to get it, but only God can

guarantee your full recovery.

One of the greatest mistakes I see people make is to speak promises to someone experiencing a winter season. People say, "He will be fine," to a mother with a dying child. We say, "Your marriage is going to recover," to a spouse fighting for his or her marriage. Listen, I am all for speaking on faith, but you cannot place hope on a circumstance instead of on God. That is false hope. When I was looking for land, I found myself trying to encourage myself by saying, "God will provide land." But I had to come to a place where I added to that, "My hope is not in the land, my hope is in Him alone." Do you see the difference? God is our Sure Thing. He is my Trump Card. He is the only thing that I can count on from day to day. Everything else is subject to Him, and when I place my hope in Him, my countenance is lifted up and I am encouraged in HIM, not in my circumstances.

David's hope in God rises him up. Not only is he encouraged, but somehow his hope encourages those around him. Remember those men who turned against him and wanted to stone him? His hope convinces them to go fight again. That is incredible! His hope and encouragement is supernaturally contagious! The presence and Word of the Lord will fill you with such confidence that others will be drawn into battle alongside of you. They will see your faith and be stirred and spurred by it. Your tenacity will collect followers, but it must come from the Lord, otherwise it will simply wear you out. A spiritual, Godly tenacity will energize you, and those around you.

Just as the Lord spoke, so it happened. They did indeed recover all without fail. You see, if the Lord says it, we must believe it! This is how we ward off the danger of weariness and faintheartedness. Spend time in His presence, seeking His Word and His direction, and then do what the Word instructs. This is where you'll find strength. Faith will fade in the waiting if you are not intentional to feed it. By the mouth of the Living God you are fed and your spirit soars.

> *"But those who wait on the Lord shall renew their strength; They shall mount up with wings like eagles, They shall run and not be weary, They shall walk and not faint."*
> *Isaiah 40:30*

℮ PRAYER PRACTICE

Lord, teach me to come to You for my encouragement. Beckon me into Your presence and speak Your Word into my ear. I know that it is by You and You alone that I will be strengthened and that I will rise up with newness. I pray that it is by Your Word and Your presence alone that I am filled with unction to stir me into new places and overtake the enemy and win back those who have been stolen. I thank You for the permission that You give to call for the ephod and seek Your face and Your counsel. I thank You, Holy Spirit, for Your guidance and anointing that you put within me that counsels me and directs me in every step. I hear You, I know You, and I heed You. In the sweet name of Jesus I pray, Amen.

Chapter 5 Remember the Feast

Mastering your winter is a matter of perspective. It requires the understanding and wholehearted belief that no matter what you see and no matter how you feel, there is a Divine purpose. God is always working to produce fruit in and through us.

You are not a victim of your winters. Remember *chronos* happenings are circumstantial and temporary. God is the God of the chronos. He is eternal, and His desired work trumps the lack in our winter. We must always choose to look for God. Personally, I want the most of every season, including my winters. I am not going to beg God to rush His work and what He wants to accomplish, rather I am learning to relish in His presence in the midst of it all.

I was just sharing with my staff the other day that a huge part of overcoming my depression was in learning not to fear it. You see, I could tell when I was starting to head down that path, and I would get gripped with fear because I knew the depths of the darkness and I was certain that I may not make it through another bout of it. I would immediately start to beg God to relieve me. My prayers were spurred on by fear instead of faith, and my hope was in not having depression instead of in God's sovereignty in the midst of it. When I learned that God could and wanted to work through the darkness, I shifted my prayers.

> *"Indeed, the darkness shall not hide from You, But the night shines as the day; The darkness and the light are both alike to You."*
>
> *Psalm 139:12*

The darkness of the depression did not negate the light of the Lord. It was not the depression that needed to change, I needed to change. I learned that although God did not author the depression (my own self-rejection usually authored it), He was still sovereign over it. By entering into the season with that knowledge and praying on faith that God was with me for a good purpose, the lack of fear quickly dissipated the depression. I had to choose to look at it that way and no longer allow myself to be a victim of depression.

I would be lying to you if I said that I never feel "the yuck" of that depressive spirit, but my response to it is one of boldness and confidence, because my hope is in God and His work. Therefore, I am confident that even in darkness, there is Light!

WHAT'S THE POINT?

If we know that God allows these seasons in our lives, we can confidently say that He has a reason. He does nothing in vain, but has a point to everything.

> *"My brethren, count it all joy when you fall into various trials, knowing that the testing of your faith **produces**..."*
> James 1:2
> (emphasis mine)

Let's stop the verse there for a moment. Three keys words. First, we are to count it all "joy." I think it is important to note that joy is not the same as pleasure; meaning I don't have to be walking through a pleasurable season to have joy. Wow! That is an incredible thought. Do you know how freeing it is to tell people that they can be joyful even though little Johnny is on drugs, or their spouse is leaving them, or their kiddo is failing classes, or they have cancer? The world has somehow convinced us that if we are joyful in the midst of trial that must mean we don't care or that we are in denial. But God says to "count it all joy" during such times.

Second, notice the word "knowing." It doesn't say we are to "think" or even "hope," but to "know." There is confidence in the word *knowing*. When I am in a meeting, and I throw a fact out on the table, I better be sure of it before I use the phrase "I know." The Greek word for this denotes to "perceive, understand or to be acquainted with." When I understand the heart of God and I am acquainted with His ways and His Word, I have a knowing. Sometimes people ask me how I know things about situations. Sometimes I can say something specific about what God has spoken or shown me, but sometimes I just say, "There is just a knowing in my knower." The Spirit of the Lord in me has made it so, and I know that I know. He wants us to walk through our winters with a resounding knowledge that He is producing.

That brings us the third key word "produces." The word here is often translated as "worketh." It means to "perform, accomplish or achieve; to bring about or to fashion." There is a glorious outcome that God desires through every trial. Through our winters He accomplishes that outcome while fashioning us.

> *"But let patience have its perfect work, that you may be perfect and complete, lacking nothing."*
>
> *James 1:2*

God is not willing that we would be incomplete. He wants to mature us into fullness. The KJV reads it like this: *"That ye may be perfect and entire, wanting nothing."* Discontent is warded off by this knowledge. He loves us enough to continue to grow us and multiply our fruitfulness. Just like a gardener, He does that through the pruning process of trials and tribulations... or winter seasons!

> *"Being confident of this very thing, that He who has begun a good work in you will complete it until the day of Jesus Christ."*
>
> *Philippians 1:6*

I can honestly say that the last thing I want to do is enter into a winter season, but one of my first heart's desires is to have my intimacy with Him intensified. It is my confidence that I can embrace a winter with joy and not with dragging fingernails.

PRAYER PRACTICE

> *God, I thank You that I can be confident in knowing that you are completing me and maturing me through all things. I rejoice in my trials because I know that You are unwilling for me to fall short of all You have created me to be. I don't always like what I am walking through, but the knowledge of Your Presence and Your love will see me through and I choose to let that be good enough for me. I*

*thank You that You have never let me go, and given
me the easy way out, even when I have begged You
to. You are all-knowing and I rest in that in every
season. In the name of Jesus I pray, Amen.*

JOSEPH'S EXAMPLE

I want to close this section by reflecting on the story of Joseph in Genesis 40-42. This whole story is about feasting in a famine. Joseph was a man who sought the Lord through many unfair seasons of winter. During those times, he continued to rely upon the heart of God. His hope was in God alone. He knew that God was continuously at work, even while he was in a pit and in prison. God had shown Joseph his destiny years before. It was the knowledge that God had a plan for Joseph and was using all things for his good that kept him moving forward with trust in God's plan.

His moment finally came when he stood before Pharaoh and was divinely able to interpret Pharaoh's dreams. Pharaoh's dreams foretold of a winter that was yet to come—a famine that would hit the land. Seven years of plenty (fall) and seven years of famine (winter). God spoke to Joseph, showing him how to gird up the land so that they would not starve in their famine. The Bible says that Pharaoh put his signet ring on Joseph's hand, signifying authority throughout the land. You see, our divine interpretations of our seasons will gain us authority to choose as well.

God reminds us through Joseph that we are guaranteed to walk through winter seasons. It is a part of the natural cycle. We have learned that death always precedes life and therefore should not be feared or avoided. There was nothing Joseph could do to prevent the famine. He could not control the drought, so he focused on what he could do. He girded up and stored up the goods and fruits of God so that when the famine came, he would still be feasting, and so would those around him!

Do you see the connection here? God wants us to master our winters by feasting even in the famine. We cannot control the "weather" of our lives, but we can gird up on the goodness of God and His love and His Word. That is where we find our feast and that is how we master the winter.

"God, my shepherd! I don't need a thing. You have bedded me down in lush meadows, You find me quiet pools to drink from. True to your word, you let me catch my breath and send me in the right direction. Even when the way goes through Death Valley, I'm not afraid when you walk at my side. Your trusty shepherd's crook makes me feel secure. You serve me a six-course dinner right in front of my enemies. You revive my drooping head; my cup brims with blessing. Your beauty and love chase after me every day of my life. I'm back home in the house of God for the rest of my life."

Psalm 23 The Message

Part 2
Spring Season
Embracing New Beginnings

6 Redefining Spring

I n 2011, when I knew the Lord was calling me to start an organized ministry and get a 501c3, I knew that ministry would require a name. Every name that I thought of was either super religious, hokey, cliché, or feminine. I wrestled with coming up with a name for several weeks. I specifically remember being on a run and asking the Lord what He desired the name of this ministry to be. The phrase "Crazy8" popped right into my head. And when it did, I just knew that was it. I tell everyone that the name is both our best and our worst trait. Many people don't like it because it is "weird" or sounds "cultish" or whatever, but others are drawn to us because it is different. Whether people like it or not, it always prompts the question, "What is with the name?" My husband, Brad, and I have six kids, so I would often refer to our family as the "crazy8." Originally, that was why I assumed the Lord put that name in my mind. Simple. As Crazy8 grew and began to take form and our mission became clearer, the Lord revealed that the name was actually prophetic.

CRAZY8 PROPHETICALLY

The word *crazy* actually comes from the Greek word *existemi*. This word is used all throughout the New Testament and is translated into the English as "amazed, astounded, bewitched, and bewildered." It means to be "put out of your mind, to be beside one's self, to be in a state of wonder, insane, or crazy." It is actually where we get the term *ecstasy* from, and this is also the name of a street drug. An example of the word in context is seen in Acts 2:7.

> *"Then they were all amazed and marveled saying to one another, 'Look, are not all these who speak Galileans?'"*

This was in response to the Holy Spirit rushing in and filling the multitude causing them to all speak with other tongues. The reaction was that those who heard and saw were *amazed*. The original word here is *existemi*. They were astounded, in a state of wonder, and bewildered by the occurrence. It was unexplainable.

The number eight in the Bible means a new beginning, new order or creation, and man's true 'born again' event. To put it in order, think about the number seven and the days of creation. Seven means completion and perfection. So, seven is the completion, thus eight is the new beginning or a new start!

When the Lord spoke the name Crazy8 to me, He was prophetically showing me that our mission would be all about astounding new beginnings for people. And that is what we do! We offer people a new chance, a do-over, and a fresh start. You will notice the tagline "Astounding New Beginnings" under our logo, and now you know why.

At Crazy8, we recognize that often people get stuck in a season of winter and they are unable to move forward. Often people don't have the practical means, they don't have the spiritual tools, they don't have the emotional health, or the mentality to be able to shift and get themselves out of their winter. Our goal is to thrust them into spring! We "force" them into a new beginning through our residential program. We pick them up out of their winter, out of their poverty, out of their lack, out of their continual state of need, and we position them in a place where we can provide for them; body, soul and spirit. I want to force a spring season to manifest in hurting lives. The program offers everything new—new opportunity, a new day—but there are also new things that are required of the ladies. They pick up new skills, new habits, new ways of thinking, new coping skills, new ways of speaking, and new ways of making choices. Everything is new and it's a place they have never been before.

I often tell people that our housing program is like being put back into the womb for two years. We tear strongholds down and rebuild through the Word and His love and then spit you out into new life!

CONNECTION

This is how we would typically define a spring season. If I were to compare a spring season to a season of life, we would typically think about an adolescent. The time of life when everything is new; perhaps college is new, and they're living in a new place and on their own for the first time. Or we think of a young adult who is just coming out of college and stepping into a career for the first time. They are getting married, starting a family, purchasing their first home, or renting their first apartment. New places, new relationships. Everything that was once familiar begins to shift. The comfort of all they know is now changing. Why? Because life is running its course and the time is coming for a new thing, a new beginning... a new life.

This is the mark of a spring season; everything is new. Familiarity and comfort are no longer. And because everything is new, there are often new rules, new decisions to be made, new emotions pop up, and new thoughts need to be dealt with in a whole new way. You suddenly find yourself thrust into a learning curve.

MY RECENT SPRING

I shared with you already about the winter that I walked through in regard to searching and waiting for land. Just when I was at the point of losing hope and closing the doors on the ministry, land "popped" up along with the provision to purchase it. With that came the need to move, and move quickly. We needed to accomplish a lot in order to keep the ministry open without skipping a beat, and many of those things that needed accomplished were things I had never experienced before. In one day, my winter turned to spring and I was thrust into all new things that required a lot of learning and listening on my part. I encountered new realms of business, financing, land and development, appraisal, inspection, land survey, closing needs, insurance quotes, transferring utilities, moving logistics and much more, all along with keeping momentum to the everyday operations of the ministry. These were all things that I had never done before, at least not with a ministry! To top it all off, we only had thirty days to get it done. The stars needed to align perfectly for it to happen. I had to depend on God and expect Him for the miracle. I recall sitting in a room on May 29, 2015, the day we set the contract in motion, with several business people from our community and hearing one say, "Lisa, you are asking for a miracle." I know it was the unction of the Holy Spirit that prompted my quick response of, "Sir, I am *expecting* a miracle." I am still amazed and in awe of our God when I tell you that God superseded what they called impossible. We were shooting for a closing on June 29, thirty days to get everything accomplished, but we actually ended up closing early on June 26, 2015! Not only did God show up, He showed off... and many people were astounded by the way He moved.

The way it all happened and how fast it happened cannot be explained in human terms. After months of a long, dry winter, the timing of God was perfect and everything "lined up" in the natural "for such a time as this." But remember that winter season? Though it seemed God wasn't working, He was! There were many things that took place during that time. Connections were made, relationships were developed, funds were raised, favor was gained so that when the timing of God was nigh, everything was in place. He is an on-time God; He is never late. Though we often feel like He is late, we must remember that He is working according to a "spiritual clock," which is outside of where we dwell. This is my hope!

NEW FAITH VERSUS MORE FAITH

The newness of spring can bring feelings of excitement and adventure. On the other side, you may feel anxiety and fear of going into the depths, a place of the unknown, a place you have never been. For this journey, new faith is required. Not *more* faith, but *new* faith.

If you recall, I mentioned to you that many people had told me during my winter season that I needed to have more faith and I found it discouraging. I took those words to heart and was praying about them one night and asking God if it was true that my faith was too small or "weak." God resonated in my spirit that night saying, "It's not that you don't have faith or even enough faith, but I am requiring a *new* faith."

I often say that our relationship with the Lord is like an onion. An onion has many layers to it, but the sweetest part of the onion is the center. God continuously pulls back layers to show us new things to bring us to the sweetest place in Him, which is found in the center of His heart. He reminded me of that when He spoke to me. Just when you think you have it all figured out or you become comfortable, He will strip away a layer and leave you a bit raw or exposed for the purpose of drawing you deeper to the center of Him. This is what is happening during spring. He is stripping away all that you are familiar with to bring you into a new place that requires a new reliance upon Him. Were it not for these seasons, we would grow self-reliant and self-sufficient and our relationship with Him would not grow nearly as sweet. It is a whole new kind of faith that will multiply within you throughout the years and will bring you to a whole new level of functioning on faith.

I recall another night when the Lord spoke to me and said, "Sometimes I give you the authority to speak to the mountains, and it is moved. Sometimes I give you the strength and power to climb the mountain, and you leap and bound over it. But other times, I give you strategies, wisdom and discernment to go through the mountains."

I knew in my heart He was telling me this was one of those times. I had not encountered this kind of faith before. I had learned by experience what it meant to take authority and have obstacles moved, and to persevere through opposition and resistance, but to go *through* the mountain and trust God for directions to the other side was new. My soul begged for the mountain to be moved or for the energy to just leap over it. I tried to do things that had worked in the past, but God was doing a new thing and He was growing me into a new place in my faith through it. You see, God has different plans for different seasons, and He refines you through them.

❧ PRAYER PRACTICE

> *God, I thank You that you never become so familiar to me that I become apathetic in my pursuit to know You and hear from You. I praise You for bringing me to places in my life that require me to rely on You for every step, every decision, every move. I rejoice in seasons of the unknown and I trust that You will never lead me to a place where You will not accompany me and guide me. May I always remember that in every new beginning, You have been faithful. You are a God who was and who is and who is to come and I trust You to be my constant, even in the anxieties and fears of newness. I walk in the confidence of Your presence and Your love now and always. In Jesus' name, Amen.*

In this section, we will study Joshua in his spring season and learn from biblical truths how to master the spring seasons of life.

7 Building Up to Joshua

hrough every story that is in the Bible, God teaches us and instructs us for life. The stories are not just stories, they are words of encouragement that speak right into our lives today. The Word is relevant. We must not dismiss His Word as tales of people who lived long ago in a world that is no longer the same. You must realize that the characters in the Word are examples to us of how to walk victoriously through our seasons.

We are going to study Joshua. But I don't want to jump right into the book of Joshua chapter 1. I want us to look at Joshua's life as it led up to Joshua 1. This is important because I want you to see how his life connects to yours and the seasons you cycle through. Let's learn something through his life and walk away from this "story" with action items that you can practically put into play in your life.

One of the first times we see Joshua is in Numbers 13. This chapter is the pinnacle of the story of the Israelites and their great escape from Egypt. They had been in a winter season, wandering around in the wilderness for many months waiting on the fruition of the promise that had been spoken to them. Get in touch with how they might have been feeling and the thoughts that they were wrestling with and their anticipation of the getting out of that season. Finally, they had arrived! The moment that they had been waiting for and an opportunity to set eyes on what they had been believing God for all along. Imagine the depths of their weariness and faintheartedness, and then imagine how their souls were lifted up when Moses announced, "The time has come!"

"And the Lord spoke to Moses, saying, 'Send men to spy out the land of Canaan, which I am giving to the children of Israel; from each tribe of their fathers you shall send a man, every one a leader among them.' So Moses sent them from the Wilderness of Paran according to the command of the Lord, all of them men

who were heads of the children of Israel."

Numbers 1:1&2

According to the word of the Lord, Moses sent one man from every tribe ahead to check out the land where they were to settle. Among these men was "Hoshea the son of Nun, whom Moses called, Joshua" (Numbers 13:16). Moses instructed them to bring back fruit. He wanted them to bring evidence of the life and abundance of the land that had been promised. We don't really know why, but in my humanness, I can certainly speculate that Moses may have wanted (or even needed) to see proof. Or possibly he knew that the Israelites needed the proof to boost their faith. Or maybe he just wanted confirmation that he was leading them on the right track. Again, I don't really know, but I do know what it is like as a leader to need evidence from God that I am not leading my staff astray, or to want to present evidence to them to stir them up for the mission.

"Then they came to the Valley of Eshcol, and there cut down a branch with one cluster of grapes; they carried it between two of them on a pole. They also brought some of the pomegranates and figs."

Numbers 13:23

"Then they told him, and said: 'We went to the land where you sent us. It truly flows with milk and honey, and this is its fruit.'"

Numbers 13:27

And indeed, there was evidence. The spies brought back visible proof that God was right! However, despite the Word of God and the evidence of the accuracy of His Word, there was another visual that they had that superseded the blessing of God.

"Nevertheless the people who dwell in the land are strong; the cities are fortified and very large; moreover we saw the descendants of Anak there..."

Numbers 13:28

YOUR BUT VS. GOD'S BUT

Right on the heels of displaying visually and declaring verbally the fruit that God had in mind for them, they spoke the word "Nevertheless," meaning, "But." I think too often we let our "buts" override the "buts" of God. I have heard it said, "God's 'but' is always bigger than your 'but.'" It is a great statement that bears much truth. When we face our giants, our obstacles, our fears, our winters, or even our springs, we must train ourselves to always say, "But God..."

The Israelites let their "but" be bigger than God's "but." As a counselor, I see this challenge among His people all the time. I will tell people what the Word says and give them counsel in regard, and often, people respond, "But..." "But you don't understand... But you don't know my husband... But you have never lived there... But you haven't been through what I have been through... But there is no money... But I can't..." Our "buts" in life keep us in the place of excuse and prevent us from moving forward. There are many facts in your life that can explain where you are at and the challenges that you are facing, but when you choose to allow them to be your excuse, you limit the power of God and your power to choose. You reject the authority that God has given you to move beyond your circumstances and your past and step in to the milk and the honey of His promises. It is healthy to be realistic and honest about your life, but you must learn to follow all that up with, "BUT GOD!"

℮ PRAYER PRACTICE

God I am in the middle of chaos in my life, BUT You are my peace. I sense nothing but darkness, BUT You are my light. I feel weary, BUT You are my strength and my rock. I don't feel like I can go on, BUT You say I can do all things through You. My knees are challenged to stand and my arms feel limp, BUT You give me legs to scale a wall. You lift me and set my feet high upon a rock. I feel like I am getting my butt kicked by the enemy, BUT You say the enemy is crushed as fine dust beneath my feet. I feel like the whole world is opposing me, BUT You

say that if You are for me, who can be against me? God, I believe your "buts" over mine. I will not give in to my circumstances nor will I let them give me an excuse to quit. Despite how I feel and what the world says, You are with me. I believe, receive and will walk in it.

TWO MEN TAKE A STAND

The spies came back and chose fear instead of faith and their fear infiltrated the entire camp except for two men, Joshua and Caleb. The Word says that these two men, the youngest of the spies, took a stand for the promise of God and declared to the assembly their belief in God to deliver them into the land. This seems like it would be an easy task because we know the end of the story. We know the Scriptures and we know what God did and how He did eventually deliver them into the Promised Land.

I believe Joshua and Caleb knew the end of the story too, not because they had read the story, rather because they were confident in the heart of God. They believed based on faith, not sight. They had confidence in what God had said and they believed it to the point of being willing to move on it. There is indeed a difference between speaking our faith and moving on our faith. I think it is important to learn that it is faith PLUS works (action) that equals the promises of God.

Sidetrack with me for a moment and let's chase down this concept biblically. So often we see people lean to one side or another in regard to faith and works. There are those who simply think I can *pray my way to the promise* and others who think they can *work their way to the promise*. Scripture demonstrates both. From what I see, it demonstrates starting on faith and adding work to faith... not the reverse!

Think about Hannah. She was downcast because of her barrenness and went to the temple to pray. The priest, Eli, encourages her that the Lord will grant her a child.

"Then Eli answered and said, 'Go in peace, and the God of Israel grant your petition which you have asked of Him.' And she said, 'Let your maidservant find favor in your sight.' So the

woman went her way and ate, and her face was no longer sad."

1 Samuel 1:17 &18

Hannah received a word or a promise from God through Eli and it stirred up faith in her. Thus the Word was mixed with faith. Her countenance was lifted and she went away encouraged. Look at what happens immediately after. Hannah's faith compelled or prompted her to act upon the promise.

"Then they rose early in the morning and worshiped before the Lord, and returned and came to their house at Ramah. And Elkanah knew Hannah his wife, and the Lord remembered her."

1 Samuel 1:19

The word *knew* here means they were one with each other. They were intimate and had sexual relations. Compare it to Genesis 4:1, "Now Adam knew Eve his wife, and she conceived and bore Cain..." Hannah added action to her faith. She literally went home with a newness of confidence and was intimate with her husband. In this case, faith plus work literally birthed the promise.

I think too often we sit around, holding onto a word from God, never moving or acting upon it. Then we wonder why God isn't coming through on the promise.

Listen, someone can bless you with a field that promises fruit, and you can pray over it, anoint it, lay hands on it, blow the shofar over it... but until you decide to add seed to the ground and work the field, you will never get fruit. You have to work the promise on faith! This does not mean I am going to work for God and add faith to my own work, but rather, I hear from God and add to it a work.

"What does it profit, my brethren, if someone says he has faith but does not have works? Can faith save him? ...Thus also faith by itself, if it does not have works, is dead."

James 2:14 &17

During my recent winter season, the Lord spoke the phrase "active rest" to me. He taught me how to rest and wait actively. This meant that I was not going to stress about finding land or "make it happen" by using my own tactics or manipulations. I also wasn't going to just sit around and wait for God to just drop the land in my lap either. I had to be active and intentional. On faith, I was to keep pressing in and looking for land. I was to keep in contact with realtors and examine any open door that He brought. My faith was not enough, I had to add activity to it!

> "For a dream comes through much activity, And a fool's voice is known by his many words."
>
> *Ecclesiastes 5:3*

The King James Version says, "For a dream cometh through the multitude of business..." Joshua and Caleb demonstrated this biblical concept in their willingness to combine the dream of the Promised Land with action. They knew that in order to reap the fullness of their deliverance that they must be willing to move. We will be discussing this a lot more in the season of fall.

Track back to Joshua and Caleb. I want you to see the amount of faith that these two had and their readiness to jump out of the winter of the wilderness and into the unknown of the spring.

> "But Joshua the son of Nun and Caleb the son of Jephunneh, who were among those who had spied out the land, tore their clothes; and they spoke to all the congregation of the children of Israel, saying: 'The land we passed through to spy out is an exceedingly good land. If the Lord delights in us, then He will bring us into this land and give it to us, 'a land which flows with milk and honey.' Only do not rebel against the Lord, nor fear the people of the land, for they are our bread; their protection has departed from them, and the Lord is with us. Do not fear them.' And the entire congregation said to stone them with stones. Now the glory of the Lord appeared in the tabernacle of meeting before all the children of Israel."
>
> *Numbers 14:6-10*

These two were so faith-filled that they rose up to the point of being willing to be stoned by all their brethren. They had a spiritual perspective and saw what the others didn't see. They were not so focused on the natural that they missed out on the spiritual happening. They recognized God's timing. Therefore, they were confident in God's presence and His ability to protect them and make their enemy as bread to them. They had faith! Yet we know that this event started a forty-year winter season for the Israelites, which included Joshua and Caleb. This fact gives credence to the concept of God often teaching a new faith through a winter. It was not because they had no faith or not enough faith that they were plunged into a winter. That was indeed the case for the majority of the Israelite camp, but not so for Joshua and Caleb. Rather, they were encountering a new faith.

I am trying to drive this point home because I don't want you to feel like you are being punished by God for a lack of faith. The wrath of God was satisfied on the cross. That is what the Word of God tells us and you must know that winter seasons are not always because you lack faith or because God is "unhappy" or "upset" with you. This is a false teaching and is foul thinking. God is always motivated by love and it is His love that stirs up faith in those who are struggling through a winter season. We must remember this in our winters, as well as when we set out to encourage others who are in a winter.

Am I saying that there are not consequences that we often have to reap because of choices that we have made? No, I am not. There are absolutely consequences to our choices, good and bad. But His mercy triumphs over His judgment every time (James 2:13), and it is still His love and kindness that will bring us into and out of those consequences. Remember, it is the kindness of the Lord that leads us to repentance. (Romans 2:4)

Be encouraged that your winter is not because God is mad at you or angry at you or trying to punish you. Nor is it necessarily because you don't have faith or enough faith. Joshua has enough faith to take a stand to the point of taking a stoning; yet he still had to endure a winter. Just as there are natural seasonal cycles, there are also spiritual seasons that God intends us to cycle through. It is important that you understand this and stay focused on God's heart of love for you. In **all** things He is desirous to refine you and bring you into your fullness! He loves you so much that He continuously wants to deepen and intensify His intimacy with you.

There is a false precept out there that winter seasons are a result of God punishing us, but that denotes the idea that God is mean or wrathful, and He is not. He is first and foremost love and He is always motivated by love.

PRAYER PRACTICE

> *God, I recognize that Your heart is love. Your Word says that "God is love" and that You bear the very essence of love. Were it not for You, I would not know love, but because of You, I know perfect love. I thank You and praise You that You love me so much that You are unwilling to just "leave me alone," but that You are continually refining me. I thank You that no matter how much I desire to be near to You, that it does not compare to how much You desire to be near to me. Thank You, thank You not just for expressing and demonstrating love, but for being love. Amen.*

DEATH BEFORE LIFE

If you recall, in the winter section we learned that death always precedes life and that we can cling to that truth in our winter seasons, knowing that spring always comes after winter. We see that in the life of Joshua.

For forty years, Joshua served next to Moses in the wilderness and no doubt developed a close relationship with him. However, in order for the Israelites to enter into their new land, or spring, Moses had to die. Consider not just the winter season of their wilderness, but also now the winter season of death. The Bible tells us that the Israelites mourned for Moses for thirty days, which was their tradition.

> *"And the children of Israel wept for Moses in the plains of Moab thirty days. So the days of weeping and mourning for Moses ended."*
>
> *Deuteronomy 34:8*

The initiation of Joshua as leader could not occur until the death of Moses had taken place. Again, we see life and newness coming out of winter.

"Now Joshua the son of Nun was full of the spirit of wisdom, for Moses had laid his hands on him; so the children of Israel heeded him, and did as the Lord had commanded him."
Deuteronomy 34:9

Right on the heels of Moses' death, we see a new beginning...a spring! Stepping into this position for Joshua and for the Israelites probably wasn't that easy of a transition. A whole nation mourning, feeling lost... literally without the man who had led them through forty years of wandering in the wilderness. Everything that God spoke to them was through Moses. He was their lifeline to their God and the only one they had ever known. They got to see the Lord work through Moses in forms of signs, miracles, and wonders. I can't imagine the loss they felt...not only of Moses, but of the hope of the promise. Not only was Moses gone, but in Joshua chapter 3, we learn that the cloud and pillar of fire that they could visibly see was now gone too. This was the visual imagery of the Lord's Presence that led them. Everything was changing and becoming new. All that was familiar was shifted. The way God comforted them, gave them shade from the sun and warmth in the nights, the way He fed them, the way He spoke to them... it was all gone. Truly this was a new beginning that no doubt stirred up fear and anxiety, right when they were about to enter into new territory with a new leader. I would likely be thinking, "God this is when I need to know you most. I need you to be familiar to me and now you seem to be changing all the "rules."

This so depicts the feelings and challenges that come with a spring season. No matter how prepared we think we are, we are never fully prepared. I believe that is how God likes it. I say often that God is not looking for the adequate, He is looking for the available. Thank You, Jesus! It was important for us to look at Joshua's foundation and history so we can understand the big picture of the spring seasons and appreciate the challenges that he was about to face as we turn the page from Deuteronomy 34 to Joshua 1.

8 Stepping into Spring

The moment Joshua had been waiting for, the time for which Moses and the Lord had groomed him all those years is now. Now? In the midst of all this loss and chaos and confusion? Yep! Can you imagine how poor Joshua felt? We know that Moses had appointed Joshua "for such a time as this." He is the one the mantel of leadership was passed onto and with it came an anointing of a spirit of wisdom to lead and discern. He was it. The one to lead this new generation into their new land. Can you imagine? A new people, a new land, a new leader, a new manifestation of the Lord… talk about pressure! And to top it off, he was filling Moses' shoes. That is not exactly the leader I would want to follow. Those are some pretty big shoes to fill.

CONNECTION

We need to grab a hold of this because this is where Scripture becomes relevant and alive to us. This is where we connect and learn in a way that is practical to our everyday lives. We need to learn how Joshua received instruction from the Lord and how he made it through and was able to conquer the Promised Land. We can get directives from the Lord through this story in the Word. We can be encouraged and empowered by putting ourselves in Joshua's shoes and learning from him. Don't just read the Word; connect the Word to you and where you are at.

Scripture doesn't say this, but I am willing to bet that there were several other men coming out of the woodwork saying, "I am the one who should take us into the Promised Land. I am to be leader. I could lead better than Joshua." I don't know that to be true, but I do know the heart of man and the way it works, so I think it is likely a fair assumption that in the midst all of this there was jealousy and pride to contend with. I certainly have no doubt that in the company of those Israelites, there were doubters and naysayers. Are you connecting now? The moment when you are stepping into your dream of ten, twenty, thirty, or forty years and many around you try to step in front of you or keep you from taking your place. I am just keeping it real! There is likely not a single person that cannot relate to being in a place of great excitement and anticipation of what is around the corner, the pinnacle of your dream coming true, the moment you have been waiting for, or the breakthrough you have been longing for. And there, all around you, are the party poopers. They are cynical and discouraging, and they aren't quiet about their thoughts and opinions. They are quick to point out all the challenges of your situation and why you might not be quite ready. They will even twist Kingdom principles by saying things like, "Well, if it's the Lord's will," or "Remember, either way, God is in control, " or "Just don't get ahead of God." The statements could go on and on. I know because I have heard them all! Most are said with good intention, but some with a spirit of jealousy and pride. This is where we can learn from Joshua and how he was encouraged during this season.

WHERE'S OUR ENCOURAGEMENT?

In the midst of Joshua's greatest hour, who was there to encourage him, to spur him on? His mentor who trained him and took him everywhere was now dead. Picture the discipleship between Moses and Joshua. Consider that everywhere Moses went Joshua was with him; gleaning and learning. It was through serving and assisting Moses that Joshua was equipped and made ready. I talk extensively about this concept in my first book *Discipleship: From Information to Execution*. Consider these verses.

> "So Moses arose with his assistant Joshua, and Moses went up to the mountain of God."
>
> *Exodus 24:13*

> "As the Lord had commanded Moses his servant, so Moses commanded Joshua, and so Joshua did. He left nothing undone of all that the Lord had commanded Moses."
>
> *Joshua 11:15*

There was camaraderie between Joshua and Moses and now

it was lost. The leader who had always encouraged and directed Joshua was gone, leaving Joshua to enter into the height of his career alone.

We are going to walk right through Joshua 1 to gain insight on how to master our spring seasons and weather the storms that often come in the spring or our new beginnings.

"After the death of Moses the servant of the Lord, it came to pass that the Lord spoke to Joshua the son of Nun, Moses' assistant, saying: "Moses My servant is dead. Now therefore, arise, go over this Jordan, you and all this people, to the land which I am giving to them—the children of Israel. Every place that the sole of your foot will tread upon I have given you, as I said to Moses. From the wilderness and this Lebanon as far as the great river, the River Euphrates, all the land of the Hittites, and to the Great Sea toward the going down of the sun, shall be your territory. No man shall be able to stand before you all the days of your life; as I was with Moses, so I will be with you. I will not leave you nor forsake you. Be strong and of good courage, for to this people you shall divide as an inheritance the land which I swore to their fathers to give them. Only be strong and very courageous, that you may observe to do according to all the law which Moses My servant commanded you; do not turn from it to the right hand or to the left, that you may prosper wherever you go. This Book of the Law shall not depart from your mouth, but you shall meditate in it day and night, that you may observe to do according to all that is written in it. For then you will make your way prosperous, and then you will have good success. Have I not commanded you? Be strong and of good courage; do not be afraid, nor be dismayed, for the Lord your God is with you wherever you go."

Joshua 1:1-9

Notice that it was God Himself addressing Joshua directly. God was quick to fill the loss of Moses by giving Joshua some "one on one" counsel and encouragement. I love this because I need to be reminded of this. I am going to be honest; I love to be encouraged by man. I love when people affirm and spur me on and I think that it is quite possible, that if I were Joshua, I would have been in search of a person to encourage me or to pray with me or to affirm me. This is natural and how our culture has raised us up. But I think we would do well to trust the Lord to encourage us more directly. Too often we rely on the people around us to feed and lift us. God Himself is not ever void of encouragement. Here we see exactly that. God spoke directly to Joshua. We can be sure that in our times of loneliness and loss of counsel, God Himself is adequate to show up and speak directly to our hearts. At the end of each day, whose word do you rely upon most to keep you lifted up? Man's word is a perk, but it cannot be your sustenance. God's Word is eternal and will bypass your soul and speak directly into your spirit, thus transforming your soul, that is, your mind, your will, and your emotions. Ultimately, that is what we need.

As a counselor and minister, I am very careful not to speak encouragement from my own words. I must use His Word. First, I want those to whom I am ministering to know that I am speaking truth to them, not just puffing them up or flattering them. Why would I look to my own thoughts of them, when it is God's thoughts of them that impact the heart? When I continue to speak His Word over someone, I force his or her soul-realm to line up with the spirit. I am speaking truth into them, and I can do it with authority and confidence because it is the Word, not just my opinion. We often call this "imparting the Word." It is amazing to watch someone shift in that moment. The Word truly is a sword that separates our feelings and thoughts from truth.

> *"For the word of God is living and powerful, and sharper than any two-edged sword, piercing even to the division of soul and spirit, and of joints and marrow, and is a discerner of the thoughts and intents of the heart."*
>
> *Hebrews 4:12*

I teach a class on our grounds called "Read and Execute the Bible" and the first half is all about reading and discussing the relevance of a passage. The second half is where we practice praying that truth over ourselves, and also into each other. So we speak truth into each other thus shattering lies that would keep us from living His fullness. We want to be practiced on how to use the Word as a weapon in our own lives, and also in the lives of others.

His Word bears much power and we use it!

A CALL TO ACTION

Take note of all the verbs found in Joshua 1:1-9. Verbs are action words. Just let that marinate for a moment as you reflect on the amount of directives that call for movement. This is important because it puts a large amount of responsibility or even "control" in our hands. God says "do this," and now we, the recipients of His Word, must mix the Word with faith and choose to do what He says. The Word without faith is dead. The Bible is not a dead word, it calls us into action; it calls us into movement and should compel us to "go." Too often we sit around, hearing instruction, getting information and even nodding our head in agreement saying, "Yes, that is good," then we do nothing with it. We don't know how to manifest His Word in our lives and turn it into action. Remember, your faith *plus* works equals the promise. Your Promised Land is out in front of you and I can tell you it is yours all day long, but if you want it, you have to be willing to move and enter into it.

This is part of the reason we see believers filled with all kinds of biblical knowledge not reaping the fullness of biblical promises. They have yet to learn how to take His Word and move on it. They are "hearers and not doers of the Word" (James 1:22) and thus walk around deceived, thinking that they are reaping all there is to reap, living on manna instead of milk and honey.

It is not by the word of man, but by the Word of God that you are encouraged to move forward and step out. It is His Word that gives a holy unction to go boldly where you have never gone before. Do the Word! When you sit down to read, expect directives to be given and resolve that you will do what He says. This is how you train yourself toward righteousness; making the Word useful not just for teaching, correcting and rebuking (2 Timothy 3:16).

PRAYER PRACTICE

> *God, I thank You for Your Word and that it is alive and active and that it calls me into action and greater living as well. I hear Your Word and will resolve to practice Your Word. I thank You that You*

have taught me that in doing Your Word, there is indeed much more reward in fullness and that Your fruit that is in me comes out through the activity of Your Word. Show me, Holy Spirit, how to creatively live Your Word, that Your Word would be fleshed out in my life. In Jesus' name I pray, Amen!

Move forward knowing that God desires to compel you into action. Continue to watch specifically for how God encourages Joshua and hear His Word as a Word to you so that you can master your spring.

Chapter 9   The Action Plan

We are going to take a deeper look at Joshua 1:1-9 and pull out some specific action items. I often use that term with my staff when we are conducting meetings, so we each have a clear understanding of what is expected of each of us in order to keep the mission running and accomplish our goals. I like to say that if I don't walk out of a meeting with an action item, it should have been an e-mail. I also use that term when I am ministering or preaching. I let the listeners know that they will walk away from the message with actions items, or ways to put the Word into practice. If they don't, then what good is the message? I want more than information; I want execution. That is what we are going to do with Joshua and the words God spoke to him. Again, it is the Word mixed with faith plus a work (action) that equals the promise! And we want to reap the promise of mastering our spring so let's break it down.

ARISE AND GO

"Moses My servant is dead. Now therefore, arise, go over the Jordan, you and all this people."

Joshua 1:2

After a season of resting and being still, God commands Joshua to move through the resounding statement, "Arise and go!" The Lord's timing is always perfect and He continuously shifts things in linear time to prepare for spiritual happenings. This is why it is so important that we not get stuck in our linear or *chronos* circumstances. Joshua watched and waited for God to say, "Now!" and he knew that God was working outside of all that he could see. He was content, but not complacent, because although he expected God for the promise, He waited on the spiritual season, which was God's perfect timing.

ARISE

The word *arise* in Hebrew means to "become powerful, to stand, or to be established." Get ahold of what God is saying here and make it personal. There have been many times in my life I have heard the Lord say, "Lisa, I want you to rise up, I want you to take your stand and be established. Be a firm foundation and be resolute. Be immovable and be determined. Be tenacious and make your face like flint. Stand like an iron pillar and be unwilling to be persuaded otherwise." That is what God said to Joshua here. He reminded him of who he is and his divine assignment.

A new beginning that takes you into a new state or new place will often demand you to live with a new level of power and authority. Know that God will anoint you with that power and authority in the form of an assertion that will gain you favor with man. This is for the purpose of accomplishing His mission. God will call you to step into that with confidence and power, which comes from the knowledge that He is with you and before you. Remember, this is HIS mission and you are on mission for Him. You don't have to defend or fight for the mission, you simply have to believe in it with a resounding confidence.

I once had someone in our community ask me if anyone ever told me, "No." At first I laughed and thought "Of course," but then as I really thought about it, I realized it was rare. So I took advantage of the question to share how God works by answering, "I typically try to only ask for things that God tells me to ask for and I typically only ask them of the people He tells me to. In such cases, I am confident that God has handpicked that person and that He has likely prepared their heart for what I am asking. So, no, I rarely am told no. God honors those who listen and follow His leading." It was a great moment. What this man noticed was favor, and I was quick to affirm that favor and point it back to God and His hand on the mission I am on.

This is what it looks like to arise! It is to be confident in who you are and where God is taking you and how He is using you. When I know that I am on God's track, then I know He is paving the way and all I have to do is stand and be established. I can walk in authority knowing that God is in me, guiding and leading me in all that I do. I heard it once said that to rise up is to come into one's self. I believe that it accurate. Joshua knew who he was and what was due him and what was due the Israelites. To rise up and step into the Promised Land was to finally come into the fullness of their identity as children of God. With that knowledge comes power and authority!

GO

The word *go* used here in the Hebrew language means to "pass over, overflow, to pass beyond, or to pass by or through." Webster's English definition is "to move from one place or point to another; to travel, or to leave or depart." There is a difference between activity and movement. God moves us from one place to another, whether physically, emotionally, mentally, or spiritually. He is a God of movement and advancement and His activity has purpose. We will talk a lot more about activity versus movement in the summer season, but for now, know that the word *go* is a strong directive that compels a clear moving from one place to another. It speaks of an accomplishment or arrival on the other side of our activity. This requires intentional activity that has the motive of moving from one spot to another in your life.

How many of you can honestly say that from last year till this year, there has been growth in your life spiritually? If you cannot say that, somehow the spiritual cycle that God has in mind for you has been squelched. We are created to increase in the likeness of Christ so there should be an automatic growth taking place in your life.

> *"But we all, with unveiled face, beholding as in a mirror the glory of the Lord, are being transformed into the same image from glory to glory, just as by the Spirit of the Lord."*
> *2 Corinthians 3:18*

The phrase "from glory to glory" here means an increase, growth, or expansion. This is more than pointless activity. It is advancement or forward movement.

Reflect back to this idea of production in the life of a believer. Consider a rose bush. We have knock-out rose bushes in our back yard, and every fall we cut them back. We perform an "act" that will cultivate the organic nature of the bush, which is to produce more fruit the following spring. And no matter how far back we cut those branches, as long as the root system is intact, not only will that bush bear fruit; it will bear more fruit. Every year, these bushes get bigger and produce more and more flowers. This is the natural process of the bush. It is the law of creation. The DNA in that seed forces the bush to continue to increase year after year.

I have seen people cut down large trees, but unless they pull up the roots, sprout will come out of that trunk and sometimes right out of the roots themselves. Not only do we believe this natural concept, we *expect* it!

We should expect the same of ourselves spiritually. The DNA of Jesus Christ is in us and if we abide in Him, we will not only bear fruit, but we will automatically increase in fruit. If you do not see growth in your life, you should ask yourself why. "Why am I stagnant, why am I stuck?"

It is interesting to me how many places I am invited to go back to minister to year after year and how some people grow, while others deal with the same issues year after year with no spiritual growth. I am not talking about dealing with the same circumstances, but rather the same internal battles or sins. They are still mourning, or they are still depressed, or they are still bitter, or they still have need for attention and drama in their lives. Can I be honest and say that I am strongly bothered by that? There is an organic spiritual process in their lives that is squelched and that deeply grieves me. The Word says that if we are deeply rooted in the river of God, everything we do is productive and produces life—even in our winters!

> *"Blessed is the man Who walks not in the counsel of the ungodly, nor stands in the path of sinners, Nor sits in the seat of the scornful; But his delight is in the law of the Lord, And in His law he meditates day and night. He shall be like a tree. Planted by the rivers of water, that brings forth its fruit in its season, whose leaf also shall not wither; And whatever he does shall prosper."*
>
> *Psalm 1:1-3*

Ezekiel 47 speaks of a river that flows from the temple. The chapter illustrates the depths of this river and the fruitfulness found along its bank, no matter the season. And the fruit is not only productive, it is useful and effective. This river is a representation of the Holy Spirit and the fruit He produces in our lives when we settle in His depths, no matter our season.

> *"Along the bank of the river, on this side and that, will grow all kinds of trees used for food; their leaves will not wither, and their fruit will not fail. They will bear fruit every month, because their water flows from the sanctuary. Their fruit will be for food, and their leaves for medicine."*
>
> *Ezekiel 47:12*

Loop this back to the directive to, "Go!" God is a God of intentional movement and production. It is His nature to multiply and advance. Being created in His image, we have the same unction and desire to move and go within us. This is a part of our purpose and what we were created for.

◉ PRAYER PRACTICE

> *God, I recognize that You have created me for growth and that You have set me up to prosper. I declare that because I am deeply planted in Your love and Your Spirit, I bear much fruit in every season. I know that in this day, I will be productive, I will multiply, and that nothing in my life is a loss. I expect to increase in my likeness to Jesus and to exemplify that likeness in all that I think, feel, say and do. I praise You for Your seed that is in me that causes me to walk in fullness and produce in abundance. You have accomplished all things and it is established... I am the planting of the Lord and I bear fruit! In Jesus' name I pray, Amen.*

BE STRONG AND COURAGEOUS

Joshua 1:6 reads: "Be strong and of good courage, for to this people you shall divide as an inheritance the land which I swore to their fathers to give them."

This is our next directive. It is important to know that in times of newness, there will be an inclination to waver in confidence. We will tend toward wavering in our emotions, our thoughts and our faith, and in those times, our resolve will be a little less "resolved." God knows that Joshua will encounter such times as he moves into the new land and He wants to gird Joshua up so that he can master his spring. This directive is to encourage, which means to be infused with courage. It is like God Himself is taking a giant, heavenly syringe and inoculating Joshua with confidence so that he won't fall ill to fear and discouragement. God is literally imparting courage into Joshua. This is the power that the Word of God holds. It is a supernatural inoculation of truth, life, and health that protects you from the viruses and diseases of the world.

STRONG

The word *strong* in Hebrew means to "strengthen, prevail, harden, be strong, be firm, be resolute, or make bold." I love the word *resolute*. To be resolute means to be admirably purposeful, determined and unwavering. This requires a mindset that is fixated on the outcome you want with an unwillingness to be deterred from that outcome. It means, "I am hard-headed!" I also love the example of this resolve we see in the New Testament woman with the issue of blood.

> *"For she said, 'If only I may touch His clothes, I shall be made well.'"*
>
> *Mark 5:28*

This woman determined ahead of time what was going to happen. If she even just touched the clothes of Jesus, she would be healed. She was confident to the point of saying, "I SHALL!" Not "I might," or "I hope," or "I think," but "I SHALL." This was a resolution that she made in her mind and heart and she was fixed on that resolution no matter the obstacles. The Amplified Bible reads, "She kept saying..." meaning there was repetitiveness going on. She repeated her determination over and over in her head and heart. It was that determination and resolve that caused her to press through the crowd and cross cultural barriers. It was that resolve that gave her the strength to overcome all the things that stood against her and the previous messages that she had been told. She actually took ownership over her own destiny and determined the outcome.

Strength is a mindset, and it is a necessary mindset as you enter into a season of change. Remember, God said this to Joshua before he stepped into the promise. He shifted Joshua's thoughts so that they were set on what is right and true; He got Joshua's mind on the promise and nothing else. Like Joshua, when you know God is calling you into something new, resolve must be determined beforehand.

COURAGE

The word *courage* in Hebrew means to "be strong, alert, brave, stout, bold, solid or hard." It also encompasses the idea of confirming oneself and being persistent. Look at the incredible picture we get of standing on a solid rock with no chance of losing your footing or slipping. It means that I have such solidity within me, that though I walk through the trials and the hazardous conditions of life, I am not shifting or persuaded by the elements, I am resolute and solid internally.

This strength and encouragement came from the Word of God. It is so imperative that you learn to rely and lean upon the Word of God and its directive. His Word should drive you and move you forward.

"For the Word is living and powerful."
Hebrews 4:12

There is power in His Word to impart action and compel us into movement. It is by His Word that we get the unction of the Holy Spirit to be confident, strong, bold, and courageous.

The devil will try to steal your confidence and trick you to question yourself. He knows the impact that we all can be for the kingdom through the power of the Holy Spirit and he does NOT want us to agree with that power. Once you are a believer in Christ, he can't steal your salvation, so he moves to plan B, which is to keep you from knowing and believing who you are and the power you hold through Christ. He will beat you down until you settle in defeat and discouragement, which is the opposite of encouragement. In Hebrew, the word *discourage* translates to mean "to weaken the hands of." This is not of God. If you are not intentional to hold on to the confidence in what you know God has said, you will lose heart.

> *"Therefore do not cast away your confidence, which has great reward. For you have need of endurance, so that after you have done the will of God, you may receive the promise."*
> Hebrews 10:35&36

Is this not what the woman with the issue of blood did? The word *endurance* here means "the capacity to continue to bear up under difficult circumstances." Your confidence is not of your own strength. It comes from His Word. It is in the knowledge of who He is and who He has created us to be that we are girded up and confident. This knowledge comes by the very mouth of God... the Word of God. We would do well to learn to reflect upon His Word regularly for strength just as we would return to our table for food for nourishment. Remember, the woman with the issue of blood "kept saying..." She did not just hear His Word, but she kept on repeating it and meditated upon it all the way through the manifestation of it.

The Word goes beyond the soul and stirs up the spirit. This is more than just the adrenaline push you get through really good "pump up" music you hear before a big game. Man can emotionally pump me up and excite me, but God is the one who compels me and inspires me. Only the Holy Spirit can give me the supernatural boost that supersedes any adrenaline rush this world or my flesh can provide. I can't press on and endure during trials and opposition solely on adrenaline, the fumes of my soulish emotions, or man's excitement. I must have the unction and inspiration that only comes by the fire of the Holy Spirit. The very Word of God fuels this fire.

"Be strong and of good courage." God isn't just speaking to Joshua, He is speaking directly to you and me today so that we can be girded up as we enter into our spring seasons.

℘ PRAYER PRACTICE

> *God, I receive your injection of courage and strength in my life that comes through Your Word. I thank You that it is Your Word that compels me and fills me with fire. I thank You that you do more than just excite me, but You inspire me. I do not cast away my confidence, and I expect the reward of endurance. I expect that I will receive the promises that You have spoken and I run with those promises in mind and I will not shrink back. In Jesus' name, Amen.*

This transitions right into the next directive.

CLING TO THE WORD

> *"Only be strong and very courageous that you may observe to do according to all the law which Moses My servant commanded you; do not turn from it to the right hand or to the left, that you may prosper wherever you go. This Book of the Law shall not depart from your mouth, but you shall meditate in it day and night, that you may observe to do according to all that is written in it. For then you will make your way prosperous, and then you will have good success."*
>
> *Joshua 1:7&8*

There is so much to learn from these two verses in regard to edging into a spring season. In a season of change and newness, we head into the unknown, and it is important that we let His Word and His Presence be our guide.

> *"His Word is a lamp to my feet and light to my path."*
>
> *Psalm 119:105*

I love this word picture. God likens His Word to that of a lamp. The lamp He refers to is not like the lamp we have on our end tables. He was referring to an oil lamp that was lit by a flame of fire. These lamps would illuminate approximately three feet in diameter.

If you were holding an oil lamp, only about a foot and a half in front of you would be lit up. That is about one step! God is saying that His Word will lead you one step at a time, so not only is it important to walk in accordance to His Word, it is important not to get ahead of God. Holding to His Word doesn't just mean doing what He says, it also means not doing what He hasn't said. Even Jesus said, "I say only what I hear the Father saying, and I do only what I hear the Father doing." He did nothing of His own initiative, but rather followed the leading of the Father.

Can I be honest and tell you that I struggle with getting ahead of God? I sense the Lord showing me something in the spirit and my mind tends to immediately try to figure out how I can make it happen. Sometimes knowing a lot of people and having the contacts where you can fix or manipulate things can be a stumbling block. I have too often "birthed Ishmaels" because of that. We must learn to let God set the pace and wait for HIS appointed time on everything. The real Isaac is worth waiting for; God's conception, God's birth, God's time.

God impresses this same concept by stressing our position spatially to His presence through Joshua 3. The Bible tells us in John 1 that the Word of God became flesh in the form of Jesus, so we know that the Word and His presence are inseparable.

> *"And He commanded the people, saying, when you see the ark of the covenant of the Lord your God, and the priests, the Levites, bearing it, then you shall set out from your place and go after it. Yet there shall be a space between you and it, about two thousand cubits by measure. Do not come near it, that you may know the way by which you must go, for you have not passed this way before."*
>
> *Joshua 3:3&4*

God told Joshua not to get ahead of Him or His presence. Joshua would not know where to go, which way to turn, or the timing in which he should move except by the movement of the Ark. The Hebrew word for *passed* in this passage includes the idea of *going beyond*. That is what a new beginning is. It is going beyond any place you have ever been. It is stretching out further and extending beyond any boundary that has previously been in your life.

It is important for us to cling to His presence and His Word. This sets us up to master our spring. How do we cling to Him? Again, we can see some very clear verbs in this passage that we can take as action items.

CLINGING TO THE WORD: SPEAKING

"This Book of the Law shall not depart from your mouth,"
Joshua 1:8a

Many versions use verbiage such as "keeping His Word upon our lips." This means actually speaking His Word out loud. I am not sure we understand the depths of how powerful it is to actually speak the Word of God. If we did, I am confident we would speak it more. My daughter has recently been challenged in memorizing her math facts, so it was recommended by her teacher that we use flash cards and have her say the facts out loud as she reads them. It has been amazing how much it has expedited the memorization process. However, when it comes to speaking His Word, we are not just more likely to memorize it, we loosen life in the process. The Word is alive and active so we can't even begin to imagine all that happens in the spirit realm as we speak it. This is why God commands Joshua to do so. It is not just so that it is on the front of our mind, but it shifts things in the atmosphere as we move into our new beginning. Our voice throws the Word out in front of us and grants us passage through our opposition and obstacles. Remember the letter the king wrote to the governors of all the surrounding regions in the book of Nehemiah?

"...let letters be given to me for the governors of the region beyond the River, that they must permit me to pass through till I come to Judah."
Nehemiah 2:7

Just as a letter from a natural king has power to grant passage, so the letter of The King has power to grant passage.

I believe this is the purpose of the exhortation given in Psalm 34:1.

"I will bless the Lord at all times; His praise shall continually be in my mouth."

Psalm 34:1, NKJV

CLINGING TO THE WORD: MEDITATING

"This Book of the Law shall not depart from your mouth, but you shall meditate in it day and night."

Joshua 1:8

Not only should we speak the Word, but we should meditate upon it "day and night." To meditate means to "ponder, to study, to think or consider" over and over. If you have ever worried about something, then you are skilled at meditation. Worrying is when we ponder a problem over and over in our minds, or we talk about it continually. The Hebrew word for *meditate* includes the idea of "moaning, muttering, reflecting or pondering; to make a quiet sound such as sighing; to contemplate something as one repeats the words." In a worldly sense, we might use the verbiage, "chanting" when we think of meditation. I am not aware of anywhere in Scripture where we are told to simply read the word. We are exhorted to meditate upon it, speak it, eat it, understand it, walk in it, observe it, keep it, cling to it, consider it, remember it, hide it in our hearts, etc. Just take some time to read Psalm 119 for more.

If you are going to prosper in your spring, you must learn to meditate on His Word.

"But his delight is in the law of the Lord, And in His law he meditates day and night. He shall be like a tree planted by the rivers of water, That brings forth its fruit in its season, Whose leaf also shall not wither; And whatever he does shall prosper."

Psalm 1:2&3

When you practice for a sport, you likely run through plays over and over again. You do this so that the play becomes automatic. This is important if you are going to win when you are actually in the game. You can't always call a time-out and go back to the coach to confirm the play. You must have it embedded in you. That is only achieved through the repetition that is done during practice. So it is with meditating upon the Word. It becomes embedded in your heart and mind so that when you are in the heat of the game of life, you have an automatic biblical response, and you win! Yes, you master the moment!

CLINGING TO THE WORD: OBSERVING

"This Book of the Law shall not depart from your mouth, but you shall meditate in it day and night, that you may observe to do according to all that is writing in it."

Joshua 1:8

OK, this one is huge for me. My whole first book, *Discipleship: From Information to Execution*, is about moving from a place of hearing and knowing the Word to actually doing and exemplifying the Word.

"But be doers of the word, and not hearers only, deceiving yourselves."

James 1:22

"But he who looks into the perfect law of liberty and continues in it, and is not a forgetful hearer but a doer of the work, this one will be blessed in what he does."

James 1:25

These two verses tell the importance of doing the word and not just hearing it. In fact, we learn that to hear only and not do is self-deception. We see this in the Garden of Eden with Eve. She knew the word, but didn't do the word. She was given to a spirit of deception and therefore fell. A huge part of mastering our spring is doing what you know. The circumstances, fear, anxiety, opposition, unknowns, etc. will threaten to keep you from moving in the Word and putting into action what you know you should be doing and living. Doing the Word makes for a sure foundation that keeps you from crumbling and giving up or turning back.

*"Therefore, whoever hears these sayings of Mine, **and does them**, I will liken him to a wise man who built his house on the*

rock; and the rain descended, the floods came, and the winds blew and beat on the house; and it did not fall, for it was founded on the rock."

Matthew 7:24&25
(emphasis mine)

Wow! Need I say more? Come on, now! How many of us have been given counsel through the Word and have knowledge of it, but we never actually do it? At Crazy8 Ministries, our counselors are trained to give weekly, biblical assignments that will help transform our clients into doers of the word and thus set them free. We explain that a one-hour a week session does not have the power to set them free, but it is the daily practice of the meditating and doing the Word that will bring liberty. You would think they would all do it, right? Think again.

Before we cast judgment, let's consider our own actions and whether or not we are doing His Word. Are we forgiving others, are we putting the interests of others before our own, are we quick to resolve offenses, are we seeking peace, are we letting the sun go down while we are still angry, are we speaking words that encourage and edify our listeners, are we feeding and housing the widows and the poor, are we giving the thirsty water, are we making disciples? This list could go on and on. No matter our excuse, we will miss the feast if we only respond verbally to the invitation and do not show up at the wedding banquet. Many respond to the call, but few actually show up (see Matthew 22:1-14). This is what it is like to be a hearer only and never put the word into action. Notice that the end of James 1:25 says that we are blessed by what we do, not by what we know or even believe.

"...a doer of the word, this one will be blessed in what he does."
James 1:25

"Every commandment which I command you today you must be careful to observe, that you may live and multiply, and go in and possess the land of which the Lord swore to your fathers."
Deuteronomy 8:1&2

Look at the reward promised when we are careful to observe

the Word. This passage is in essence saying, "Here is why it is important for you to observe and do the word. I have a big plan for you in a new place that has abundance and blessing and you will multiply and possess much. I want to see you come into this place, but it is out of your obedience to do my Word that releases you into this place. This is your part, and I invite you to partner with Me in securing your destiny." We can stand on this passage, knowing that there is a greater purpose in our obedience than just the immediate "reward." God moves us into more life and greater possessions and our obedience forces this truth to come forth in our lives.

Speaking the Word, meditating on it, and observing to do it are very practical ways that we cling to the Word.

℘ PRAYER PRACTICE

> *God, I declare and decree that I am a doer of Your Word. That Your Spirit compels me to act upon what I hear You say. I am reminded to speak and meditate upon your Word and I write it not just upon my heart, but I write it upon my lips. Your Word is like honey dripping out of my mouth and like a fire shut up in my bones and I am compelled to speak of You and Your Word continually. You have caused me to be constant in my meditation of Your statutes and I stand on them as my rock and my solidity. In Jesus' name, Amen.*

Hang with me here as we explore a few more directives given to Joshua. There is a lot to learn from him and how God prepared him for spring.

REMEMBER HE IS WITH YOU

> *"Have I not commanded you? Be strong and of good courage; do not be dismayed, for the Lord your God is with you wherever you go."*
>
> *Joshua 1:9*

Remembering is more than just having a memory; it is *choosing* to remember. There is a big difference. I can't necessarily control my memories, but I can choose to forget, and I can choose to remember. To choose to remember that God is with you is what I call "practicing His presence." This means I am going to be intentional to acknowledge His presence over and over (meditate) in all things at all times.

I am known to occasionally just speak out loud at any given time that I know God is with me. This is powerful because it boosts my confidence and infuses me with courage. "If God be for me, who can stand against me?" (Romans 8:31)

God reminds Joshua of His continued and constant presence; that no matter where Joshua goes, God is with Him. God knows that the reminder of His presence will be important as Joshua heads off into his new beginning. I am willing to bet that Joshua was there when Moses cried out in Exodus:

> *"Then he (Moses) said to Him, 'If Your Presence does not go with us, do not bring us up from here...for how then will it be known that Your people and I have found grace in your sight except you go with us?'"*
>
> *Exodus 33:15&16*

Joshua learned the power of God's presence and the importance of choosing to remember and meditate on it. When God's presence is your focus, everything else becomes miniscule and you are able to stay fixed on the mission, much like the woman with the issue of blood. His presence makes our plan sure and unshakeable and causes us to walk in victory.

> *"Fear not for I am with you; Be not dismayed, for I am your God. I will strengthen you yes, I will help you, I will uphold you with My righteous right hand."*
>
> *Isaiah 41:10*

Look at the resounding, "I will" spoken to us in this passage. It is the "Yes and amen" of God's presence and the promise of peace that it brings. When I am in fear or dismayed, to choose to remember and meditate on His presence is to choose to shift my focus on truth, and that truth will set me free from my fear.

℮ PRAYER PRACTICE

I acknowledge Your presence and that You are with me in all things and at all times, therefore, I have not fear. If You are with me, who could stand against me? Because of Your presence that surrounds me, I am bold and I am confident and I know that I am loved. Thank You, Jesus for your camaraderie in all that I do. In Jesus' name I pray, Amen.

SANCTIFY AND CULTIVATE

"Sanctify yourselves, for tomorrow the Lord will do wonders among you."

Joshua 3:5

I would be remiss if I did not mention this directive given in chapter 3. The word *sanctify* in Hebrew means to "consecrate, prepare, be hallowed, be holy, be separate." It's the idea of being made ready. When you know a new beginning is coming, you must intentionally sanctify yourself. I liken this to how one would prepare soil and make it ready before planting seeds. To set a seed up to grow and prosper, one would cultivate the land to make it fertile. To *cultivate* means to break up any hardness and prepare the soil. This would also involve removing any weeds that could potentially choke out the seed. Do you see the metaphor? We must be intentional to cultivate our soul by breaking up the hardness of any bitterness, unforgiveness, pride, fear, and sin. There are likely sins in our lives that pose to choke out the growth that God wants and He wants to cleanse us of those things beforehand. We must be intentional to consider our ways and be searched by the Spirit for the purpose of purging and cleansing.

"Search me, O God, and know my heart; Try me, and know my anxieties; And see if there is any wicked way in me, And lead me in the way everlasting."

Psalm 139:23&24

The Psalmist knew the importance of allowing and inviting the Spirit of God to examine his ways. He knew that walking in holiness was the best way to continue on a path of victory.

When we got down to the last ninety days on our old property, I believed on faith that God would come through with something big that would be right on time. Because of that, I felt Him impress upon me the importance of us all, as a staff, engaging in a time of cleansing and purging for the purpose of being girded up. I shared this imperative with the staff and encouraged them all to pray about some kind of commitment to prayer and fasting. Most of the staff took me up on the invitation and I was amazed at how God worked in us individually. I came to realize more than ever before that the strength and integrity of the ministry really relied on the individuals that made up the ministry. I was blessed at how God revealed areas to each staff member and called them to new levels of holiness and integrity. And, let me insert here that they were already grounded, mature Christians going into the fast. God, in His infinite love for each of us and in His passion for the mission, purified us deeper, thus strengthening us for the new place that was just around the corner.

God continually refines and remakes us, and with this process comes confession and repentance. It is imperative to invite His finger to point to the things in our lives that keep us from our fullness, especially when we know we are heading into a new place. You can be sure that there will be giants to be defeated as you journey through your spring, and the best way to gird up is to have a heart of repentance and sanctification.

> "But if we walk in the light as He is in the light, we have fellowship with one another, and the blood of Jesus Christ His Son cleanses us from all sin. If we say that we have no sin, we deceive ourselves, and the truth in not in us. If we confess our sins, He is faithful and just to forgive us our sins and to cleanse us from all unrighteousness."
>
> *1 John 1:7-9*

Coming into the light of the Lord is freeing and cleansing. This means bringing all your sins and iniquities out into the open before the Lord. In being honest and confessing those sins, you are girded up with His righteousness.

The devil will deceive you into thinking that because you may not have some kind of "big, overt sin" in your life, you have no need for intentional examination, confession, and repentance. Please do not dismiss the seemingly small and insignificant things in your life that will indeed trip you up and cause you to lose the battles as you journey through your spring. Joshua chapter 7 reminds us of this imperative examination through a man name Achan who stole a very "small" item from the enemy's camp (Ai) and hid it under the floor of his tent. Seems insignificant, right? I mean what is the big deal? The big deal is that in Joshua 6, they were commanded to abstain from taking any items from Ai. Although it seems like no big deal, it was disobedience, and therefore it was sin. That sin caused the entire camp to be defeated. We see God call for Joshua to cleanse the camp in Joshua 7:13.

"Get up, sanctify the people and say, 'Sanctify yourselves...'"

It is a call for cleansing and purging of all that would entangle them in their new beginning. We must walk in the light and let the Lord expose our weeds and thorns. We want to search for things hidden under the floor of our hearts. This is what I saw firsthand in my staff when we engaged in our prayer and fast. Much confession and repentance went on and the light of transparency and vulnerability disarmed the devil. This is so important in cultivating our lives personally as well. After all, every seedling needs light to grow.

ꙅ PRAYER PRACTICE

Lord, I welcome Your spirit to search and scope the depths of my heart and mind and see if there be any wickedness within me. Point out any spot or wrinkle, no matter how insignificant it may seem. I recognize that Your hand points out of love and that because of Your love, You expose darkness that is within me. I want to walk in holiness and be sanctified by You. Show me and compel me to purge

through confessions and repentance. In Jesus'
name, Amen.

CONCLUSION - MASTERING SPRING

There is so much to learn about how to master our spring season through Joshua. But just like winter, it is a matter of perspective. You must stay fixed on God and His spiritual movement in your life. A spring season can't be figured out ahead of time. You must trust God in the many unknowns that spring comes with. You can look at it with fear, or you can look at it with adventure! God created the world to cycle through seasons, which means constant change. Just like the natural world, we too are created for change and to change. Everything is continually changing, even you and I. Since this is a part of our design, we can be sure that there is a seed within us that desires change and welcomes the adventure it brings. The world will tell us that joy is found in having your future plans "secured," but God says that joy is found in adventure. Embrace your spring seasons with excitement, walk in the ways of Joshua and master every moment.

Part 3
Summer Season
A Time to Play

Chapter

10 Redefining Summer

I love summer! In our house, it is a time when our college kiddos all come home and the younger kids of course are off from school as well. We spend a lot of time at the pool, or doing various activities like going to the park, or watching sports, attending tournaments for one of the kids, or just cooking out at home. I anticipate summer and the freedom from the daily grind of school and work schedules, and the carefree spirit that comes with that "first day of summer!"

Last summer, we took our first large family vacation to Colorado and stayed in a house in the mountains. Although it was a vacation, it was filled with much activity that took us ice-skating, horseback riding, white water rafting, hiking, shopping, eating, and more. By the end of the vacation, we were all ready to come home and chill. We longed for our own bedrooms and bathrooms with our own beds and showers. Don't get me wrong, it was an incredible vacation with lots of great experiences and memories, but it was busy and filled with lots of activity.

I have found that to be true of summer over the years. Although I look forward to it each year, I also very much look forward to the end of summer. I find myself desiring to get back into a routine and have a sense of structure to my days. I need to feel a restoration of productivity in my life.

Summer is a season of high activity. There are celebrations, cookouts, and parties to attend on top of summer camps for church and sports. It is typically thought of as our "time off" or "down time" of the year. We have been trained from childhood to think of summer as a time when "school is out" which coined the phrase, "Summer Vacation." In general, I would say the mark of summer is the word vacation.

In comparing the natural summer season to a linear season in life, I would call it the prime of life. It is the crazy time of 30s and 40s when your kids are in the throes of multiple school and extra-curricular activities. All of these things and the busyness they require, though they are good, threaten to pull us away from the things that are great. Often things that are truly important. So, it is not just a season of high activity, but it can also be a season with low productivity.

I am reminded of a little booklet I once got from my mentor when my children were little and I was "out of my mind" with keeping up with the schedule of all six of my kids. Whether it was their sports schedules or their napping schedules, I was exhausted trying to keep up with what I felt like were things that *had* to be done. The booklet was called *The Tyranny of the Urgent*, written by Charles Hummel. It includes these words:

> "We live in constant tension between the urgent and the important. The problem is that the important task seldom must be done today or even this week. Extra hours of prayer and Bible study, a visit with that non-Christian friend, careful study of an important book: these projects can wait. But the urgent tasks call for instant action---endless demands pressure every hour and day.

> "A man's home is no longer his castle; it is no longer a place away from urgent tasks because the telephone breaches walls with imperious demands. The momentary appeal of these tasks seems irresistible and important, and they devour our energy. But in the light of time's perspective their deceptive prominence fades; with a sense of loss we recall the important task pushed aside. We realize we've become slave to the tyranny of the urgent."

I cannot tell you how that concept struck a chord with me personally and still does. One of the things I constantly teach others is that we have authority of our own lives and we need to practice that authority. All of us can relate to times when we have felt like our schedule was being completely dominated by things we "couldn't control." Personally, I have spent too much of my life feeling like a victim of my schedule and like I was spinning out of control with the activities of life. And much of those activities were not even my own. They were the activities of my children, or my husband, or my church, or my friends, or my ministry, etc. Trust me, with eight people in one family, things can get out of control very quickly. From meals, to errands, to chores, to random illnesses, to the dog... you name it, anything can happen! Nonetheless, I fell prey to those things and I found that I was falling victim to the urgencies of life and the important things were being left undone. It was often during summer seasons that this would happen. The seasons when we were off or on vacation were when things would get crazy busy. It is funny to me that it was during a season when school was out that I actually learned the most!

ACTIVITY VS. PRODUCTIVITY

There is a big difference between activity and productivity. I recently changed our website to reflect the productivity of our ministry more than just activity. Most websites reflect activity, but I am interested in production and outcome. I want to know what has been accomplished or what is being produced through activity, and I want to reflect the same on our website. You see, we can be an active ministry, but unless we can show production or outcome, what good is our activity?

Anyone can look busy, but being productive is very different. The devil will deceive us into thinking we are being productive, when really he is just keeping us busy and simply stealing our energy. I liken it to running on a treadmill versus running outside. I can spend an hour running on my treadmill and work up a sweat doing it, but ultimately, when I step off my treadmill, I am in the same spot as when I started. This is what can happen during our summer seasons. We get caught up with busyness and activity that yields no eternal value or outcome. There is a lack of peace in that place.

As a woman, I can say that women tend to fall into this trap more than men. Generally, we struggle to say, "no." We also have a harder time setting relational boundaries, and we love to be "martyrs." So we often find ourselves racing from place to place and trying to be all things to all people. I mean, after all, we want everyone to like us, right? And, if we are honest, we love to be needed because it makes us feel purposeful. The mark of summer is a season of high activity with low outcome, so we must be aware of falling prey to the "have tos" that we have taken upon ourselves. The truth is, many of our "have tos" really are "I *feel like* I have to," or "I *have chosen* to." These will not only overwhelm us, they will distract us from what is really important.

ACTIVE REST

Looking for land for Crazy8 Ministries was a time when I was continuously challenged by the "necessary" activity that came with searching for and viewing properties. Along with that, making all the right connections with all those whom I would need for the purchase of property and the relocating of the ministry. My days were filled with one appointment after another and I was driven by the urgency of the time constraint I was under. Until one day, the Lord very clearly spoke the phrase, "Cease from striving" to me. This immediately challenged me because I thought it meant that I was supposed to sit back and do nothing. As I reasoned with the Lord over that phrase, He further spoke the phrase, "Active rest" to me. Well, clearly this seemed like an oxymoron, but I knew He was trying to teach me something. After seeking Him and His concept of what it meant to "actively rest," I sensed Him reminding me that there was a difference between internal stillness and external stillness. What I realized was that all the activity and chaos of my circumstances were beginning to drive my internal activity and my soul was anxious and becoming very chaotic. I was experiencing high activity with low productivity or outcome and there was a lack of peace within me. God wanted to reverse that. He wanted me to rest internally and come to a place where I was at peace internally. It was out of that peace that I was driven to move. You see, I was still active, but my activity was more productive because it was driven by God and not my circumstances. Instead of needless activity, I engaged in intentional activity that was important. There were no urgencies and my anxiety was therefore gone.

MY RECENT SUMMER

After walking through the long, dry season of winter during which we waited on the Lord for property, and then the spring season of literally relocating onto the new land, I found myself abruptly enter a season of summer. Although there was a whole lot of activity that came right after the move, given that there was much to do to make the land fit for our ministry and services, the intensity and demand of the past year had completely come to a halt. The pressure was off! Thus began a season that was filled with things that we got to do, but weren't highly necessary or of the utmost importance. I attended lots of new marketing events, our numbers of tours increased, we hosted open houses, had staff cookouts, and I went back to traveling again. We painted rooms, hung pictures, shopped for furniture, and moved things around to make the new place look great. In the midst of all this activity, my own time with the Lord began to wane. My time before the office was open was spent painting instead of praying and my lunch hours were filled with luncheons instead of studying. Because my intense "need to rely" on God was gone, I slipped on my disciplines. I found myself distracted by all the things that were urgently demanding my time and attention, and I fell into apathy in my persistence of the things that were most important.

I quickly realized that my busyness was not leading to productivity, but rather my high activity was producing little outcome for me personally. Although at first there was no effect on the ministry, eventually, I saw it beginning to slide as well. Again, we were busy, but not with things that were eternally important to God.

There is much to be learned during seasons of high activity. It begins with discerning busyness from productivity. In every "chronos" season, there is a "kairos" happening. God is always working, so we know that there is purpose to summer. But, just like every other season, there are dangers and ways the enemy will try to steal what God is doing so we need to be knowledgeable and girded up. We are created to do more than just survive our summer seasons. We are created to master every moment our summers bring.

11 The Obstacles of Summer

Much like the other seasons, during a time of summer, there are things that we need to be privy to in regard to the inclinations of our flesh. Busyness and activity will come with their own set of challenges. One of those challenges is found in obstacles you will encounter that threaten to break down your fellowship with God. Now, I want to be sure to say that although obstacles or "walls" can breakdown our intimacy with God, nothing can separate us from the love of God.

> *"For I am persuaded that neither death nor life, nor angels nor principalities nor powers, nor things present nor things to come, not height nor depth, not any other created things, shall be able to separate us from the love of God which is in Christ Jesus our Lord."*
>
> *Romans 8:38&39*

There are times when we flippantly use phrases like, "being separated from God," but I think it is important that you know that even during times when you *feel* separated from God, you are not! Circumstances will lie to us and try to make us believe that God is not near, but that is never true. His presence is always with you, even when you aren't aware or are too busy to be mindful of Him. Having an understanding of this principle and choosing to believe it despite what you feel is huge in mastering your seasons. The devil wants you to feel alone, isolated, and abandoned. This is one of the first steps to a path of hopelessness, and if he can steal your hope, then you lose your unction for life. There is nothing worse than feeling completely alone or "unseen" and "unheard." God says, "I am always with you and therefore you can walk without fear."

> *"Be strong and of good courage, do not fear nor be afraid of them; for the Lord your God, He is the One who goes with you.*

He will not leave you nor forsake you."

Deuteronomy 31:6

ꝏ PRAYER PRACTICE

> *Father, I am reminded now and always that You are with me. I thank You for the peace that Your Presence brings to my life and that you are forever My companion. I choose to walk in this truth even when I don't see it or feel it. I declare and decree that even when I don't see You, You are with me. I declare and decree that even when I don't feel you, You are with me. This is what Your Word says, and I therefore stand upon it and walk in it. In Jesus' name I pray, Amen.*

This is a truth to stand upon at all times. What a solace knowing that even though we may not feel His presence, He is there. Although obstacles will distract us from His presence, they do not negate His presence. He is our sovereign trump card, which means we can count on Him for the victory in the battle of any obstacle that comes our way.

SONG OF SONGS

One of my favorite passages of Scripture is found in Song of Songs. The whole book of Song of Songs is a metaphor of our relationship with God. He is the "Lover" and we are the "Beloved," meaning, the one who is being loved. This particular passage refers to a season that comes after the dryness of winter and the freshness of the spring rains. It refers to a time when things are in full bloom and fruit is appearing, which is a picture of summer. Remember in summer we are given a "break" from the winter and spring. It is also when activity and busyness can consume our lives. This passage is a beautiful picture of how God's presence and pursuit doesn't change during those times; that although we have perhaps gotten too busy for Him, He is never too busy for us and His invitation is still given every day. His love is still chasing us down and He will stop at nothing to hold us in His arms. Let's look

106

at Song of Songs 2:8-14, although I encourage you to read the whole chapter and see this passage in context.

> *"The voice of my beloved! Behold, he comes Leaping upon the mountains, Skipping upon the hills. My beloved is like a gazelle or a young stag. Behold, he stands behind our wall; He is looking through the windows, Gazing through the lattice. My beloved spoke, and said to me: 'Rise up, my love, my fair one, And come away. For lo, the winter is past, The rain is over and gone. The flowers appear on the earth; The time of singing has come, And the voice of the turtledove is heard in our land. The fig tree puts forth her green figs, And the vines with the tender grapes give a good smell. Rise up, my love, my fair one, and come away! 'O my dove, in the clefts of the rock, In the secret places of the cliff, Let me see your face, Let me hear your voice; For your voice is sweet, And your face is lovely.'"*

THE OBSTACLES OF THE WORLD

I tend to think in pictures and poetry, so I love the word pictures used to get a point across in this passage. First, we have a picture of a lover leaping and bounding over any obstacle that would keep him from the love of his life. This is a picture of the mountains and hills in our life that threaten to block our fellowship with God. It is important that we know first and foremost that there is absolutely NO obstacle that is too big for the love of God. Life is inevitably going to present circumstances or things that we have "no control" over. Things like your car breaking down, sickness, moving, a new job, having a baby, etc. These things come with their own set of activity that we are forced to deal with. Such busyness might hinder or breakdown our fellowship and intimacy with God. However, we can rest in knowing that in such cases, God can and will overtake those things by His love and power. And, although they may be too big for us, they are NEVER too big for Him. He will simply leap and bound over them in just a step. This is the grace of God and how desperate He is to extend that grace to us. He will do anything to be one with us and there is nothing that can stop Him. His love is too strong for any obstacle that the world throws in our path and we can rest in knowing that sometimes God doesn't expect us to climb that obstacle or remove it, but rather He steps over it and finds us right where we are in the midst of it.

THE OBSTACLES OF OUR WALLS

I want to look closely at the next verse.

"Behold, he stands behind OUR wall; He is looking through the windows, Gazing through the lattice."

While there are indeed obstacles in our lives that the world brings, there are also the ones that God refers to as, "OUR walls." These are the obstacles that are in our lives because we have placed them there or have allowed them. In other words, there are times when our own choices put up walls between God and us. However, look at God's positioning in the passage when it comes to our walls, He stands "behind them... looking through the windows, gazing through the lattice." What an incredible picture of how His eye is ever upon us; that although my eye may not be on Him, His eye is on me. What a beautiful picture of His watch and care for us, even in times when we dismiss Him. I am forever amazed at the unconditional love of God. Even when we are not mindful of Him, He is mindful of us!

Even from behind our walls of fear, pride, anger, apathy, bitterness, rebellion, busyness, etc. there is an eye watching us and a voice speaking into our hearts saying, "Rise up, my love, my fair one, and come away." This is a love that is alluring us to come out from the walls that have been made by our choices, thoughts, or attitudes. Listen, God will invade the world and its obstacles to win us over, but He won't invade our will. He is a God of invitation, not invasion. Although His love is powerful, it is not forceful.

I have found that busyness will not only keep us from dealing with our current walls, we often develop new walls during seasons of high activity. Our lack of intentional care for our relationship with the Lord allows the devil to subtly put up walls and obstacles to hinder our intimacy. God is ever inviting us to be a part of what He is doing, and I think we would do well to learn that His number one invitation is to work within our own hearts. He will never overtake your own will, but instead invites you to surrender your will to His. He does this with love and kindness.

So while there are indeed obstacles that life throws at us, there are also walls that we put up or allow ourselves and it is time that we learn to discern the difference. I am afraid that we often spend too much time blaming the devil or other people or "our circumstances" for the choices we make. Until we learn the power that we have to own up to our own choices, we will forever struggle with defeat and victimization. The problem is that we spend our lives justifying why we cannot change or have no control over our lives, when in reality, we have more control than we think.

BREAKING DOWN MY WALL

I recently walked through a season where I began to feel very frustrated over continuously running late for everything. The reason I was frustrated is that I felt that I was never late because of "my own doing." It wasn't *my* fault that I was continuously late. It was because someone always needed to talk to me on my way out the door, or I had too many appointments, or my kids were running behind, or practice let out late, or I had to be two places at once, or... fill in the blank. What I realized was that for me to blame everything else for my issue was to say that I had no control over my time or my schedule. I let myself be a victim of my schedule. I know it sounds crazy, but my continued lateness began to cause me to feel defeated and discouraged.

I felt a strong conviction because I knew it was not the Lord's will for me to be late for everything. Not only did it cause me stress to spend my days playing "catch-up," it was a poor reflection of His image. Our God is an on-time God, and I know that if I am created in His image, then it is in me to be punctual. However, I was not walking in the fullness of that attribute. Moreover, I was blaming everyone else and the busyness of my schedule for it. It wasn't until I took ownership and stepped into the authority of controlling my circumstances and my time that I was able to overcome.

THE OBSTACLE OF DEFEAT

One of the things that I have found to happen when I am overwhelmed by activity is the feeling of defeat. It is the feeling that somehow my life has gotten out of control and I have absolutely no grip on my schedule. I end up at a place where I feel like my time is controlled by everyone and everything else and I spend much of my days rushing from one thing to the next. The funny part is, much of the time, these are things that are "fun" or at least supposed to be. In my haste, I get to where I can't even enjoy them because of the craziness of my schedule. My busyness affects my house and the condition of it, my time with my kids and my husband, and most importantly, my time with God.

I know there are many of you reading this who are connecting with this and thinking, "But there is nothing I can do about this." I am here to tell you, that is a lie. One of the things I have had to learn to walk in is the authority that God has given me to choose.

> *"See, I have set before you today life and good, death and evil, in that I command you today to love the Lord your God, to walk in His ways, and to keep His commandments, His statutes, and His judgments, that you may live and multiply; and the Lord your God will bless you in the land which you go to possess.... I call heaven and earth as witnesses today against you, that I have set before you life and death, blessing and cursing; therefore choose life, that both you and your descendants may live; that you may love the Lord your God, that you may obey His voice, and that you may cling to Him, for He is your life and the length of your days; and that you may dwell in the land which the Lord swore to your fathers, to Abraham, Isaac, and Jacob, to give them."*
>
> *Deuteronomy 30:15&16, 19&20*

Every day of your life is filled with choices, and God has given you the will to choose. To say that activity, busyness, and my schedule are controlling me is to hand power over to those things. It is saying that I have no control over my schedule, but my schedule controls me. In other words, "I have become a victim of my schedule." That is crazy! We have all fallen into that trap. The verse above reminds us of our power to choose, and our right to practice that power. God lays all options out before us, and if we are intentional to choose things that will bring life, there is a reward. These are the things that will feed our body, soul and spirit, and not drain us. Choosing wisely sends us to bed feeling satisfied and peaceful every night. Wise choices are ones that we won't regret tomorrow.

I often speak to teens in the public schools and I share with them that we have all been given a super power, which is the power to choose. I tell them that their choices today can actually create tomorrow's experience. We can navigate our future. God invites us to be a part of fulfilling our destinies, and it starts with every choice we make, moment by moment. My mentor has always told me that we live a victorious life one decision at a time. That is powerful. The opposite is choosing to continue down the path of defeat and victimization.

God has created us to master our seasons, even our seasons of increased activity. It is not His will for us to go to bed every night overwhelmed and exhausted. Notice that God promises in Deuteronomy that when we choose life, meaning choices that are wise and healthy, we will prosper. These verses are "if...then" statements. *If* you choose well, *then* you will add years to your life. *If* you choose wisely, *then* you will multiply and increase. *If* you choose life, *then* you will reap His blessings.

Let's be honest, falling victim to our schedules because of our inability to choose to say, "No" robs us of health, productivity, goodness, and satisfaction. We lose sleep, we are tired, we gain weight, we are stressed out, our blood pressure goes up, we are cranky, we are chaotic, and we are unproductive and dissatisfied. This is not God's design for us.

> *"Take My yoke upon you and learn from Me, for I am gentle and lowly in heart, and you will find rest for you souls. For My yoke is easy and My burden is light."*
>
> *Matthew 11:29&30*

This verse has rescued me time and time again in regard to feeling heavy-laden with busyness. God's will for us is gentle and kind. Notice this verse doesn't say there will be no burdens, but that those burdens will be light. There is a difference between the world's burdens, our own burdens we pick up, and God's burdens. I have heard it said that there is always time to do the will of God. I agree and I have clung to that truth. I would like to add that there is also enough energy to do the will of God. If I continuously feel that I am running out of time or energy, I can be sure that I am out of the will of God. I have likely added things to my schedule that were not "God-approved." These may not necessarily be bad things, in fact, they may be good, but good is the greatest enemy of best. I don't know about you, but I want to live my life with excellence and reap what is best. Why would I settle in the wilderness when I know God is calling me to the Promised Land? In such cases, I must repent and confess my loss of authority over my schedule as sin. Let's call it what it is and own up to our part. We have more control over our own lives than we think. God's very first blessing upon Adam and Eve was to have dominion. Dominate and don't be dominated (Genesis 1:28).

OVERCOMING OBSTACLES

Learning how to overcome these obstacles starts by simply recognizing them. The devil will trip us up through the drifting process that takes place as we prioritize our activities over our intimacy. Walls will build up and our victory will be stolen. As we learn to discern and recognize this, as well as stand on our authority to choose, we will begin to walk in mastery through our summer.

⚬ PRAYER PRACTICE

> God, I thank You for giving me the authority to choose and navigate my own life. I thank You for blessing me to have dominion and that I do not have to fall prey to my schedule or the activities of life. I am mindful of Your promises and I expect that as I choose in accordance to YOUR will, that I will reap blessings and experience an increase in every area of my life. I thank You for teaching me how to walk in authority and practice my power to choose. In Jesus' name, Amen.

Chapter 12 The Dangers of Summer

Just as there are obstacles that can hinder your mastery of summer, there are dangers to be aware of as well. Being aware prepares you for such times. One of these dangers is simply distraction.

THE DANGER OF DISTRACTIONS

> *"Catch us the foxes, The little foxes that spoil the vines, For our vines have tender grapes."*
>
> *Song of Songs 2:15*

At the end of the passage we looked at in the previous chapter, God beckoned us into a place of intimacy. I find it interesting that immediately after, God gives this warning. Song of Songs is extremely poetic and metaphorical. Here we see God refer to "our vines," which represents our relationship with God. It is our time, our work, and our energies that we spend with God. It is the intimacy built out of being rooted in Him, His love, and His Word. From that place, there should be an automatic production of fruit that is referred to here as "tender grapes." However, He gives a directive to "catch" the foxes, yes even the "little foxes" that would spoil such intimacy, thus stopping the production of fruit.

LITTLE FOXES

The so-called "little foxes" are those I feel most often trip us up. These are seemingly small and insignificant things that we would say are, "No big deal." They are the places we might compromise or tolerate when we shouldn't. Often, we tolerate gossip, or complaining, or things in our schedule that compromise where we should be or keep us from doing what we should be doing.

I reserve 8:00 every morning for my time with the Lord. I get

113

up, get ready, take my kids to their respective schools and get to work around eight. It is written on my calendar and everyone knows it is a "do not disturb" time for me. However, I can honestly say that almost every day, something threatens to steal that time. Well, I guess I should say there is always an option for me to compromise or give away that time. And to be honest, sometimes I do compromise. I get wrapped up in a conversation with a staff who "needs" counsel, or I have a phone call I "need" to return, or one of my kids calls me, or I "need" to stop for an errand, etc. You name it, I could come up with a reason every day to legitimately use that time doing something else. I have found that if I choose to let go of that time, after two or three days, I definitely see a loss of His fruit in my life. I feel more easily agitated, I am less joyful, or I lack in the wisdom that I need. It seems small and insignificant to fudge a day here or there, or even thirty minutes of that time, but that "little fox" has a big impact.

God intentionally used a fox as the animal to warn us, so let's take a look at the characteristics and behaviors of a fox. First, a fox is typically small to medium in size, as opposed to large and easily visible. They are nocturnal animals that hunt in the dark and are typically not seen in daylight. Their characteristics include being sly and manipulative and often are referred to as tricksters. OK, if this doesn't describe the way we get sucked into things already, listen to this; a fox uses a pouncing technique where they crouch down to camouflage themselves in their environment. Then, they suddenly leap upon their prey and use their sharp teeth to take a hold of the neck and shake it to death. I don't know about you, but I know that feeling. The moment when you realize something that appeared or presented itself as good, takes you by surprise and suddenly takes control over you. You are victimized by this event, or that commitment, or that relationship, or that task, and feel completely "shaken" up and overwhelmed to the point of losing your breath. I am quite certain that God knew what He was doing when He used the fox to warn us against things that would ruin fruitfulness and vitality in our lives.

There are things that camouflage themselves within things that are good. It is deception and the way our enemy manipulates us into what is *not* best. Remember, good is the enemy of best. The devil is savvy and sly and he will slink about in the busyness of summer waiting for you to be "off guard" and distracted by activities, and then he will pounce.

CATCH

Good news! God is not telling us to simply avoid the little foxes that would ruin our fruit, but to take hold of them and seize them. He uses the word "catch," which is often interpreted into the word "take." The Hebrew word actually means "grasp, take hold, seize, take possession." I do not have to live my life around *things*, I have been given authority to take hold of *things*. This means I can navigate my own life with boldness and not in fear.

> *"Therefore take up the whole armor of God, that you may be able to withstand in the evil day, and having done all, to stand."*
> *Ephesians 6:13*

> *"Therefore submit to God. Resist the devil and he will flee from you."*
> *James 4:7*

The Word is clear that we do not need to live our lives running from the devil or navigating our lives around him. To do such is to give him control. God is the Lord of my schedule and my choices, and I will not allow any sly fox to steal that from me. Learning to seize those little foxes will prevent the obstacle of defeat. You won't be overtaken and consumed thus becoming victimized by things you think you have no control over. Again, I will stress that you must learn to walk in the power and authority that God has given to take a hold of that which He has given you dominion over.

❡ PRAYER PRACTICE

> *God, I thank you for reminding me of the authority You have given me. I agree that You have given me the mind of Christ and that I am able to discern the devil's manipulation. I fix my eye on You and I take ownership over my life with You as my guide. Thank*

You that You bring me into the fullness of fruit. I rebuke any fox that would slip into my schedule or into my mind to distract me from You and I seize those things and cast them out. I do not desire to live a watered down life, but one that is wholly devoted and abundant in You. In Jesus' name I pray, Amen.

THE DANGER OF EXCUSES

In Luke 14, Jesus tells a parable about a great supper where many people were invited to come and eat. It is a story that He uses to explain the goodness of actually eating bread in the kingdom of God. I believe there is a difference in being a part of the kingdom of God and actually eating the bread that is in the kingdom. It is possible to be saved, but still live like the very lost. It is possible to have the redeeming blood of Jesus upon you, but still live in the guilt and shame of the past. It is possible to have the Holy Spirit within, but never reap the fullness of His fruit. It is possible that many of us, like the Israelites, spend our lives wandering about in the wilderness when God has given the milk and the honey of the Promised Land. This parable paints a great picture of the things that keep us from feasting on the fullness of our salvation.

"Now when one of those who sat at the table with Him heard these things, he said to Him, 'Blessed is he who shall eat bread in the kingdom of God!' Then He said to him, 'A certain man gave a great supper and invited many, and sent his servant at supper time to say to those who were invited, 'Come, for all things are now ready.' But they all with one accord began to make excuses. The first said to him, 'I have bought a piece of ground, and I must go and see it. I ask you to have me excused.' And another said, 'I have bought five yoke of oxen, and I am going to test them. I ask you to have me excused.' Still another said, 'I have married a wife, and therefore I cannot come.' So that servant came and reported these things to his master. Then the master of the house, being angry, said to his servant, 'Go out quickly into the streets and lanes of the city, and bring in here the poor and the maimed and the lame and the blind.'

And the servant said, 'Master, it is done as you commanded, and still there is room.' Then the master said to the servant, 'Go out into the highways and hedges, and compel them to come in, that my house may be filled. For I say to you that none of those men who were invited shall taste my supper.'"

Luke 14:15-24

One of the lessons that gets lost in this parable is that there is more to the invitation than just to respond; you must actually attend the party. Your response to the invitation does not automatically drop the feast of the supper into your lap. If you want to eat of the bread of the kingdom, you have to attend the party! One of the things I tell people all the time who volunteer at Crazy8 is that we find great value in those who just show up. There is something to be said about the faithfulness of follow through. I could rant about that for an entire chapter, but let it be said that many have faith, but I have found that the faithful are few. Too many of us come up with excuses that will keep us from being faithful and fulfilling our commitments. We don't show up, and we miss out on the feast...that simple. Although there may be valid things in your life that explain the challenges that you have, you cannot allow those to become excuses.

Notice the excuses that are given in this parable are not necessarily bad things. They are ordinary, daily things that we are all just as likely to be distracted by like work, business, accomplishments, possessions, relationships, etc. These are the excuses that are given and ultimately kept those who were invited from feasting on the goodness.

This whole parable is the passion of my life. It depicts those who have responded to the invitation of salvation, but have never actually experienced the feast of the supper that He offers. I have very little tolerance for any excuse that people bring to the table. Although I will validate their struggles, if I accept their excuses, I am allowing them to continue to walk in defeat. Excuses are like saying, "I can't help it, I have no control." Or, "It's not my fault." None of this lines up with the power and authority that God has given us. Until we begin to stop giving excuses, we will continue to miss out on the bread of the kingdom of God.

My heart is to empower people how to come into the fullness

that is due every child of God and enforce their purpose in life. This is the mission of Crazy8 Ministries and Lisa Schwarz, LLC. I am deeply saddened for the lost, but I am even more saddened for the saved that are still lost. Those who have been resurrected but still walk around with burial cloths, blind, bound and confused. We must hear the call on our lives to do more than just set the lost free, but to set those who are saved free, too. This is what it means to make disciples.

Excuses will keep you from mastering your summer. They are a danger to you and will steal the fruit of the season because they keep you stuck in your current spot and prevent you from stepping into your victory. We are overcomers in ALL things!

❧ PRAYER PRACTICE

> *Lord, may I not fall into the trap of excuses that would keep me from sitting at the table with You. I am reminded that there is no thing that is more important than responding to Your invitation, showing up, and feasting on Your goodness. You have made me wise to know better and I confess that I often fall into excuse and miss out. I receive Your grace and choose to change my choices so that You are first in all things and that there is never any excuse that would keep me from You. In Jesus' name I pray, Amen.*

THE DANGER OF APATHY

Apathy is one of the enemy's greatest deceptions toward man. According to Wikipedia apathy is "a lack of feeling, emotion, interest and concern. It is a state of indifference, or the suppression of emotions such as concern, excitement, motivation, and/or passion. An apathetic individual has an absence of interest in or concern about emotional, social, spiritual, philosophical and/or physical life and the world. The apathetic may lack a sense of purpose or meaning in their life and may exhibit insensibility or sluggishness."

Wow, talk about the opposite of how God created us to

function. I mentioned earlier that my heart is to enforce purpose in the lives of God's people. In fact the "tagline" of Lisa Schwarz, LLC is "Enforcing Purpose." God reminds us over and over in the Bible that when He put us together in our mothers' wombs, we were knit with a purpose and for a purpose. He didn't just create us physically; He created in us a plan and a vision. There lies within each of us a mission for His Kingdom, and the DNA to bring it forth!

> *"For I know the thoughts that I think toward you, says the Lord, thoughts of peace and not of evil, to give you a future and a hope."*
>
> *Jeremiah 29:11*

The word *thoughts* is often interpreted into the words *plans* or *purpose*. It comes from the Hebrew word *machashabah* which means "thoughts, device, plan, purpose or inventions." I find it interesting to note, there are a few times in the Scriptures that it is interpreted into the English word *imaginations*. So what does this mean? It means that God created us for great things! There is a vision and a dream inside of each of us that should fill us with passion and unction.

One of the first things that we do with the ladies who enter into our housing program is find out what their passion is. We ask what they have always wanted to do and give them permission to dream and reminisce about it. We want them to do that because without that, they will perish.

> *"Where there is no revelation, the people cast off restraint..."*
>
> *Proverbs 29:18*

The KJV reads it like this:

> *"Where there is no vision, the people perish."*

We can say the opposite is true as well. A vision will impart life! When we begin to see something in our future and the means by which we can obtain it, hope is instilled and passion is stirred. This causes unction for life and causes us to move forward. It is one of the fastest ways we have learned to cast out hopelessness and apathy.

People who lack vision are often apathetic. They lack motivation and struggle to become excited about life. They see no purpose to their days and are unable to see past today. Encouraging one to dream, empowering them in their purpose, and equipping them daily with steps needed to accomplish their dream can completely rehabilitate a life.

I often get the honor of speaking in schools, from elementary schools to colleges. I am typically invited in to talk about Crazy8 and what we do so I love to connect with the kids by talking about their dreams. I will start by asking what they want to be when they grow up, or what they are majoring in. Not once has any kiddo ever answered by saying they want to grow up to be an addict, homeless, or abused. I point that out to them because I want them to know that just like them, the people that we work with once had a dream, too. In a nutshell, Crazy8 is a place where we help people's dreams come true.

STIR UP THE GIFT

> *"Therefore, I remind you to stir up the gift of God which is in you."*
>
> *1 Timothy 1:6*

God has invited us to be a part of the fruition of our dreams. Paul exhorts Timothy to "stir up" that which was already in him. The phrase "stir up" here means to "kindle up, or inflames one's mind, strength, and zeal." This is the opposite of apathy. It is how we can ward apathy off in our lives. There must be an intentional stirring up of all that God has put into us. There is a difference between being intentional and having good intentions. Being intentional means I am going to turn my intentions into actions. It means being a doer and not just a hearer. Bringing forth your purpose means living with purpose. You must continually think upon and act upon your purpose. I believe this is why Habakkuk says to write our vision on a tablet.

> *"Write the vision and make it plain on tablets, That he may run who reads it. For the vision is yet for an appointed time; But at*

120

the end it will speak, and it will not lie. Though it tarries, wait for it; Because it will surely come, It will not tarry."
Habakkuk 2:2&3

Writing your vision down and making it plain on a piece of paper will help more clearly identify purpose and mission. It provides the visual you need to stimulate activity. This is a sure way to ward against apathetic dreams that never amount to anything because every dream requires intentional action.

"For a dream comes through much activity, And a fool's voice is known by his many words."
Ecclesiastes 5:3

The KJV version says, "a multitude of business" instead of activity, which frankly sounds a little less fun, if you will. It comes from the Hebrew word *inyan* which means "occupation, task, or job." The word is found eight times in the Old Testament and is interpreted into the English word *travail* six of those eight times. Fanning the flame of God's gift that is in us requires work!

God has invited you to partner with Him in the fruition of your passions and dreams. As you learn to meditate on what He has put into you, you will be compelled by the unction of the Holy Spirit to go farther, to press in, and to persevere...in every season. There will be no indifference or "suppression of emotions." You will only experience passion, excitement, and motivation. Therein lies the life that comes from having vision (Proverbs 29:18).

☙ PRAYER PRACTICE

Lord, what a blessing to know that You have put a vision within me and that all You have inspired me to do, You have also equipped me to do. I thank you for my divine assignment, and I reflect on the mission You have given me. May I be mindful every day of my purpose and the hope and life I have because of that purpose. In Jesus' name I pray, Amen.

THE DANGER OF PRIDE

After making it through a season of winter and the new beginnings of spring, coming in to summer is very refreshing. However, if we are not careful, we might take our eyes off of God. Remember, our summer season can be a time where things are a little less intense, so we are not forced to cling to God as we did in our desperation of winter and need of direction in spring. During these times, it is easy to forget the importance of who God is and all He has done if we are not intentional to reflect. When we have made it "to the other side" of winter and spring and we look back on all we have accomplished or made it through, we can't leave God out of the equation. To do so is to allow an opportunity for pride to set in.

In Deuteronomy 8, Moses exhorts the children of Israel not to forget all that the Lord did for them to sustain them in the wilderness. He tells them to be careful to continue to observe and remember how they had to rely solely on God daily. He reflects on the humility that was instilled within them during that season, much like it is with us in our winter seasons. Moses goes on to warn them about what could happen if they are not careful to continue in such intentional remembrances.

> *"Beware that you do not forget the Lord your God by not keeping His commandments, His judgments, and His statutes which I command you today, lest—when you have eaten and are full, and have built beautiful houses and dwell in them; and when your herds and your flocks multiply, and your silver and your gold are multiplied, and all that you have is multiplied; when your heart is lifted up, and you forget the Lord your God who brought you out of the land of Egypt, from the house of bondage; who led you through that great and terrible wilderness, in which were fiery serpents and scorpions and thirsty land where there was no water; who brought water for you out of the flinty rock; who fed you in the wilderness with manna, which your fathers did not know, that He might humble you and that He might test you, to do you good in the end—then you say in your heart, 'My power and the might of my hand have gained me this wealth.'"*
>
> *Deuteronomy 8:11-17*

122

Moses was a wise man in his warning. He fully recognized the tendency of man to puff ourselves up in our own accomplishments. The phrase "when your heart is lifted up" means the "exaltation of inner man or a boasting of self." Interesting to note that one of the original temptations in the Garden of Eden involved the pride of life. Satan appealed to Eve's flesh by telling her she could be like God, "knowing good and evil" (Genesis 3:5). It was also one of the temptations that Satan brought to Jesus in the wilderness.

"Again the devil took Him up on an exceedingly high mountain, and showed Him all the kingdoms of the world and their glory. And he said to Him, "All these things I will give You if You will fall down and worship me."
Matthew 4:8&9

Jesus, however, did not fall for it like Eve did. John also reminds us of the danger we face in regard to the pride of life.

"Do not love the world or the things in the world. If anyone loves the world, the love of the Father is not in him. For all that is in the world – the lust of the flesh, the lust of the eyes, and the pride of life – is not of the Father but is of the world."
1 John 2:15

The root of the Greek word for pride here actually means "an empty pretender." Isn't that a classic characteristic of pride? Pride keeps us pretending, stuck with a mask on. Acting like we have got it all going on because we are too proud to admit otherwise. And don't forget the word "empty." Not just a "pretender," but an "empty pretender." There is no emptier place that when we are stuck playing a part that is not who we really are. The inability to be real or genuine with others, or frankly even with ourselves, is a very empty place that will spiral us into a pit of isolation and loneliness. I know that I struggled with that as a mom for many years. Feeling like I had to measure up to every other mom and play parts that weren't true to who I was. I had to pretend like I was good at things like sewing, cooking, or baking. These things were not and are still not my sweet spots, but for a long time, pride kept me pretending. I wanted to fit the mold and wasn't mature enough in my walk with

God to admit humbly that I was not good at those types of things.

"For My people have committed two evils; They have forsaken Me, the fountain of living waters, and hewn themselves cisterns-broken cisterns that hold no water."

Jeremiah 2:13

A cistern is a large underground container that is used for collecting and storing water. When you find a cistern, you expect to find water, but a broken cistern would be found empty. God is likening our self-reliance, depending on our own strength for resource, to that of a broken cistern. We dig and dig with the promise of finding the sustenance of water, but in the end it is empty. In such cases, the trap is that you must keep digging more and more, resulting in exhaustion that leaves you depleted.

Pride traps you into relying upon yourself and not on God. Satan will do whatever he can to keep you from depending on God. He is a glory stealer and he will allure you into self-glorification. This is not because he loves you, but rather because he hates God and will do anything to keep God from being glorified. The number one way God is glorified is through His people. This was the very purpose of our creation: to reflect the glory of the Lord. When we boast of our own power and the works of our own hand, we dim the light He has put within us, squelching His presence and hindering our own fullness. Pride steals our potential. It is a nasty trap that will keep us living as "an empty pretender" instead of reaping the freedom of transparency and honesty.

I heard it once said that there is no limit on what God can do if you don't care who gets the credit. While this sounds unfair, there is actually much freedom in that mindset. And, personally, I have found it to be true.

Jesus said that if He were to glorify Himself, that His glory would mean nothing (John8:54). Even Jesus recognized that to honor Himself or magnify His own power or works would amount to nothing... it would be empty.

When we are at a place of reaping and prospering, we need to be sure to remember that it is only because of God's hand in our lives. By praising God and reflecting with thanksgiving, we will ward off the danger of pride in our heart.

PRAYER PRACTICE

Father, I hear Your voice exhorting me to reflect always on all You have done for me and the guard that it puts upon my heart. I desire for Your name to be glorified and never my name. May Your name be renown in my life and may Your hand be seen and known through my actions. I am Yours and my life is Yours...do with it what You want and use if for Your good and for Your glory. I wrap myself in a cloak of humility and I ask You to show me any signs of pride in my life that would keep me stuck in the emptiness of my own ways and resources. In Jesus' name I pray, Amen.

CONCLUSION - MASTERING SUMMER

We know that God is always at work in our lives, so we need to expect fruit no matter where we are or what season we are in. God will cycle us through seasons, which will include summers, where we find a chance to reprieve, refresh, and relax. It is an opportunity to bask in the sun and soak up the reward of accomplishments. So what is God teaching us and how is He refining us and maturing us in this season? I believe the answer is consistency and self-discipline. During our mountain top seasons, we praise God. During our valleys, we cling to God. In those in between times of everyday life that I personally find it difficult to stay the course. Our summer seasons should train us to walk consistently. During those seasons God affords us the opportunity to develop healthy spiritual habits that become non-negotiable. We must learn to pursue Him and stir up our intimacy because it is the right thing to do and how we grow spiritually healthy.

"I am the vine, you are the branches, He who abides in Me, and I in him bears much fruit; for without Me you can do nothing."
John 15:5

To abide means to "remain, to tarry, to endure or last." It means "not to depart." Think of the phrase "My sweet abode." This is the place where you find rest and safety, a break from the chaos of life. It is one thing to run to the vine in crisis or praise, it is another to learn to abide even when you don't "feel" you have a need or purpose to.

Summer allows you the opportunity to learn how to step outside of the soul. It is a season where you aren't necessarily emotionally drawn to God, but is something you choose do and becomes who you are. When you learn to stay consistent and faithful despite the urgencies, activities and busyness of summer, you have learned how to master the season.

Part 4
Fall Season
Rise Up and Harvest!

Chapter **13** Redefining Fall

We have come full circle in this book. We started with winter and we end with fall. From desolation and famine to life and abundance. I can't think of a better finale than that! Anyone who knows me knows that I want to see everyone come into the fullness of life and reap abundance.

Naturally, fall is known as the season of harvest. The dryness of winter is over, the planting and work of spring is passed, and the vacation of summer has ended. Farmers live for the fall because they get to reap the fruit of their labor and their diligence and patience "pays off." The mark of fall is abundance, the season of much fruit.

In comparing the natural fall season to the linear season of life, I would say fall is like that of the latter years of life. When, hopefully, you are retired and reaping the fruit of years of laboring and you are able to sit at the table and feast on the goodness of that fruit. Ideally, the dream is that in the latter years, your kids have moved out, your mortgage is paid off and you collect some sort of retirement. Many people spend their lives dreaming about what they hope for in retirement. Things like moving south, or living in the mountains, or traveling around the world. In other words, reaping the fullness of life and living in the lap of luxury, or abundance. However, you and I both know that this is not a guarantee in the natural.

CONNECTION

We have learned that each natural season reflects a spiritual season. We can be sure there is a spiritual fall season that we cycle in and out of as well. Much like in nature, it is a season of abundance. When we have persevered through winter, journeyed through the new beginnings of spring, and learned consistency and constancy through the activities of summer, we will eventually come into the abundance of fall. We have survived the droughts, sowed the seed of His Word, and practiced nurturing that seed through discipline. It is the fruition of the promise spoken to us in Galatians 6:9.

> "And let us not grow weary while doing good, for in due season we shall reap if we do not lose heart."

This is not a suggestion, but a promise. A promise that we shall—not might—shall reap if we "faint not." The abundance of fall can be counted on because it is biblical and a part of the spiritual cycle that God created for us. The abundance in the spiritual fall season is more secure than that of the linear. Although we dream about such abundance in our latter years, there is no guarantee. Spiritually, we are guaranteed. Natural seed can fail us, and monetary seed can fail us, but His seed promises a return.

> "For as rain come down, and the snow from heaven, And do not return there, But water the earth, And make it bring forth and bud, That it may give seed to the sower And bread to the eater, So that My word be that goes out from My mouth; It shall not return to Me void, But it shall accomplish what I please, And it shall prosper in the thing for which I sent it."
>
> Isaiah 55:10&11

Isaiah teaches that God's Word produces. A farmer can go out into a field and sow seed, but he will never get a 100% return. Some of the seed will sprout, but some of it will not. This is not the case with the seed of God's Word. It will never return void. It shall accomplish and therefore I shall reap if I continue on. In Hebrew, the word *void* here means "in empty condition, in vain, or without effect." What a promise we can stand on. I don't know about you, but there have been times when I have felt like I've sown God's Word in vain, either in my own life or in the life of another. It is times like that when I declare what is true.

PRAYER PRACTICE

> *Father, I know Your Word says that wherever the seed of Your Word falls, it produces. I stand on that truth and expect fruit in my life and the lives of those in which I am sowing and I refuse to let what I see or how I feel dictate or deter me from this truth. I praise you for Your biblical principles and I stand and act upon them and I thank for the continual cultivating of every Word that is within me. In Jesus' name I pray, Amen.*

PRINCIPLES OF REAPING AND SOWING

I once learned about the farming and gardening laws of reaping and sowing seed. Though the laws were taught in regard to the natural, I have found them to be true spiritually as well. It has been helpful for me to remember and apply them when understanding what it takes to reap a harvest. There are some basic principles to help us see the bigger picture of how things work in the spirit. As we saw from Isaiah, no matter what, you will reap! In this chapter we explore additional principles to build on this truth.

YOU REAP WHAT YOU SOW

You won't just reap—you reap what you sow. If I sow corn seed, I will reap a corn stalk. Seems very simple and makes sense right? We get it in the natural, yet we miss it spiritually. Paul shares the same principle in Galatians.

> *"For he who sows to his flesh will of the flesh reap corruption, but he who sows to the Spirit will of the Spirit reap everlasting life."*
>
> *Galatians 6:8*

Just like sowing corn, reaps corn; sowing in flesh, reaps flesh. In every action, thought, or attitude, you sow seed, and out of that seed fruit will come and it will be a direct product of what you sowed. I like to demonstrate this principle with my clients by showing them two pots, one marked "flesh" and the other marked "Spirit." I then give them a handful of seeds and tell them those seeds represent all the choices they have made for the week previous to our visit. Then we go through every decision and "assess" whether or not it was a spiritual decision or a fleshy one. One by one, we fill the pots. I remind them, either way, you will get fruit. The question is what kind of fruit... the fruit of the flesh or the fruit of the Spirit? This helps the client to recognize why they reap what they do and reminds them that they have the power to navigate more than they think. For example, a client might come in with an increase in their struggle with depression. I might ask questions from what kind of sleep they have been getting, to what their thought life has looked like, to whether or not they have been making good eating choices. I might ask them if they have sown seed into the biblical assignments that I had given them or if they have been engaging in other coping mechanisms. Every answer they give is a seed, and at the end of my questioning, inevitably there are typically more seeds in the "flesh" pot than in the "Spirit" pot. The client is then able to see that they are simply reaping what they had been sowing. It is empowering to know that we can be a part of what fruit we bear through our lives, simply by what seeds we choose to sow.

YOU REAP MORE THAN YOU SOW

Another principle is that you will always reap more than you sow. If I sow one corn kernel, I will reap a corn stalk. My one seed multiplies into many. A farmer expects that with every seed he sows, he will reap more out of that one. Again, simple and easy for us to believe and understand naturally. The same is true spiritually. Jesus likens a heart that has received the Word of God as being one that is fertile and calls it "good" soil.

> *"But he who received seed on the good ground is he who hears the word and understands it, who indeed bears fruit and produces; some a hundredfold, some sixty, some thirty."*
> *Matthew 13:23*

"They sow the wind, And reap the whirlwind."

Hosea 8:7a

Because of this principle, we can and should expect that with every seed that we sow spiritually, there will be an increase. However, it is not just an increase of fruit, but a multiplication of seed. This is the process of regeneration and how God created the world to increase life. We must understand this spiritually as well as naturally. The good news is that for every small seed we sow to the spirit, we will reap larger amounts spiritually. The bad news is that for every small seed we sow to the flesh, we will reap in larger amounts as well. Remember those small seemingly insignificant foxes that will spoil the fruit of the vine? This is why. Even the "smallest" sinful choice in your life will not only produce a consequence that is larger than the original choice, but that consequence will bear more seed with the potential to produce or bring forth more sin. Consider what James is saying in regard to this principle.

"But each one is tempted when he is drawn away by his own desires and enticed. Then when desire has conceived, it gives birth to sin; and sin, when it is full-grown, brings forth death."

James 1:14&15

Every action produces an increase in our lives and it is to our advantage to use that spiritually. With every spiritual action we make, we can count on an increase of spiritual return.

YOU REAP LATER THAN YOU SOW

Everyone knows that you never reap at the same time as you sow. There is always a time of waiting. Again, it's simple and we get this naturally! So why can't we grasp this spiritually? Our faith tends to be short lived because we yearn for proof or evidence. So we sow and sow and continue in the righteousness of God, but when we don't see fruit, we lose heart. This brings us right back around to Galatians 6:9.

"And let us not grow weary while doing good, for in due season we shall reap if we do not lose heart."

Note the phrase "in due season." The word, "season" is the word *kairos*, not *chronos*. We learned in chapter 1 that *kairos* is spiritually driven timing, and *chronos* is related to chronological time.

When we sow, even spiritually, we are still doing it within a linear (chronos) time. However, the season in which we reap is in accordance to spiritual time... God's time! If we are not wise to this concept, we will weary ourselves thinking our spiritual sowing is in vain. Do not look for your spiritual fruit within natural time. God's timing is perfect and you must not faint while you wait for it.

Fall season is what you have been waiting for! It is when the planting and cultivating pays off. Knowing these principles will help you in your understanding of how the seasons work, both naturally and spiritually.

PRAYER PRACTICE

Father what a blessing to understand that in all of creation, You are teaching me something about who you are and the way you work. I pray that You would open my eyes that I would see and be wise to all You have made known through Your ways. I thank You Lord, that You have made wisdom readily available and that through your natural seasons I can learn about how my life cycles spiritually. May I respond and live according to Your principles and may I not grow faint in waiting for the abundance that is due me because or Your Son. I recognize that my inheritance is in Him and that in Him there is much fruit and blessing. I will continue sowing to Your Word, sowing to Your love and sowing to Your Spirit knowing and believing that in Your perfect timing, I will reap! In Jesus' name, Amen.

Chapter 14 Purposes for Fall

There are purposes to the fall season beyond harvesting the fruit. Let's explore them together.

PREPARATION

A very important purpose of fall is to be a time of preparation for winter. Fall is God's provision for the coming hard times and how He intends to sustain us during the droughts and famines. This is why it is so important that we learn to harvest and bring the fruit in, which we will examine in the next chapter.

> *"He who has a slack hand becomes poor, but the hand of the diligent makes rich, He who gathers in summer is a wise son; He who sleeps in harvest is a son who causes shame."*
> *Proverbs 10:4&5*

To sleep through our harvest and miss out on the fruit is to lack wisdom. A wise man knows the cycle of life and thinks beyond today and into tomorrow. At Crazy8, we call that "thinking long" or the "thriving mentality." Because many of the ladies we work with have been in poverty or homelessness, they have learned to do just enough to get them through another day. The urgency of their immediate needs has overtaken their ability to think beyond today. By eliminating those urgencies through the provision of food, shelter, transportation, childcare, etc. we free them up to stop living in survival mode and start thriving. This starts in their minds and the ways they think. It is a huge obstacle that we have to overcome by continually reminding them to "think long" with every choice they make. The ability to plan and prepare for tomorrow through the choices they make today takes much wisdom and self-discipline.

We must understand that we are cycling through spiritual seasons, and that with every season of abundance, there will be a season of dryness, a season of desolation, a season of drought, or a season of famine. We can count on that because we know that life brings us in and out of winters. If we understand that fall is not just about reaping, but also preparing for winters, we will be diligent and wise to collect and reserve. Consider the ant that does such.

> *"The ants are a people not strong, yet they prepare their food in the summer."*
>
> *Proverbs 30:25*

The word *summer* here in Hebrew denotes a season of fruit. All of nature understands the importance of preparing for winter and so should we.

JOSEPH'S PREPARATION

Think with me about the story of Joseph in Genesis. God gives man (Joseph) insight into what was yet to come. Pharaoh had a dream that revealed two seasons that were coming, a season of abundance and then a season of famine. In this story, we see the cycles of seasons, and how we will go in and out of times of abundance and in and out of times of famine. These are our falls and winters. Joseph, understanding the knowledge of these cycles that are coming, demonstrates wisdom and stewardship in his counsel to Pharaoh.

> *"Now therefore, let Pharaoh select a discerning and wise man, and set him over the land of Egypt. Let Pharaoh do this and let him appoint officers over the land, to collect one-fifth of the produce of the land of Egypt in the 7 plentiful years. And let them gather all the food of those good years that are coming, and store up grain under the authority of Pharaoh, and let them keep food in the cities. The food shall be as a reserve for the land for the seven years of famine which shall be in the land of Egypt, that the land may not perish during the famine."*
>
> *Genesis 41:33-36*

Joseph is wise with these words. He recognizes the provision that God is giving to them before they need it and he knows that they need to be good stewards of the abundance they are about to receive.

JEHOVAH JIREH

I want to take a moment to look into the name Jehovah Jireh. This is the name that Abraham gave to God in Genesis 22 in the scene where the ram was caught in the thicket. The ram was the provision that Abraham needed to fulfill the offering that God was requiring. In short, the name means "My Provider," but it actually encompasses more than that. It means "a God who goes before and provides in." This is huge. It means that God is never caught off guard in regard to our needs. He is out in front of us, not just preparing the way, but supplying *for* the way. Although there was a point in the story where Abraham sees the ram, we don't actually know how long the ram had been there. I believe the ram was there long before Abraham even knew his need for an offering. You remember, Abraham thought that Isaac was to be the offering. God had something else in mind and the provision to fulfill the offering was already in place. What a beautiful demonstration of how God works and His heart of provision for His children.

So it was with the story of the Israelites. God already had a ram hidden in the thicket in the form of seven years of abundance. God is in the business of supply. He is never in demand because He "owns the cattle on a thousand hills" (Psalm 50:10). He doesn't just supply for our today, He supplies for tomorrow as well. Through understanding the cycle of these seasons we learn that often what He gives today actually provides for tomorrow. This is why He calls us to be good stewards and practice preparation.

Again, at Crazy8, one of the challenges that we face with the residents in their survival mentality is that they are unable to think beyond their immediate needs. They often lack in the ability to save their money in preparation for tomorrow. This comes from living in poverty and the poverty mentality that keeps them thinking that they need to spend everything they have as quickly as possible so they don't lose it. It sounds backwards, I know, but it is true. One of the hardest times for us is when a client receives a tax return because it is so hard to get them to use the large amount to plan for their future instead of gratifying their immediate needs or wants. I say this to say, if we find ourselves in constant lack, we should ask ourselves why. There could be many reasons, but one of them may simply be poor stewardship and lack of preparation.

Because Joseph understood the concept of stewardship, the Egyptians and his own family were able to feast during the famine. So it is with us. Don't just limit this principle to the natural, I am talking about the spiritual season as well.

GIRDING UP

We should store up spiritually. I believe this is what it means to "gird up." The phrase *girding up* comes from an Oriental practice where they would bind up their long, flowing garments closely to their bodies in preparation for a journey or before engaging in any work. They realized that flowing garments would impede them in their movement or work. Spiritually, this translates to mean that not only will I have material things (stuff) that will need to be gathered up and made ready, but my entire being must be gathered up and ready too. There should be no "dangling participles" in my life or things hanging out there flowing in the wind.

> *"Therefore gird up the loins of your mind, be sober, and rest your hope fully upon the grace that is to be brought to you at the revelation of Jesus Christ."*
>
> *1 Peter 1:13*

The Message says it like this: "Get your mind in gear." Having your mind in gear prepares you for the winters that are coming. You are better able to conquer the dryness and famine of that season when your mind is girded and focused on His blessings. In a season where abundance is great, steward His blessings well and gird up with His goodness. When I am filled up with His blessings, I am better prepared for the battle of winter.

> *"Finally my brethren, be strong in the Lord and in the power of His might. Put on the whole armor of God that you may be able to stand against the wiles of the devil."*
>
> *Ephesians 6:10*

We see the same concept here in Ephesians. Paul tells the Ephesians the importance of being prepared in advance—before the battle. He is saying, "Gird up and be ready! Guard yourself and dress yourself with truth."

I once had a student ask me if I was really that disciplined to intentionally "put on" the armor of God every morning. And without a thought I responded, "Sweetheart, I don't ever take it off!" God has taught me to be always found suited up and ready for whatever season is coming. He truly has provided us resources to stand in the face of every battle.

God is a good steward of every resource and therefore so should we be. Wisely stewarding the abundance of our todays means that we are mindful of tomorrow and the needs of our tomorrow. Now, don't hear me saying that we should worry about our tomorrow. What I am saying is that I believe that God has given us what we need for our tomorrow in our today. Remember, He is out in front of us and knows the needs of our future and is faithful to provide for those needs in our today.

SEED FOR SPRING

Another purpose of fall is to collect seed for spring.

God is a God of multiplication and He is forever increasing and growing that which He created. For that purpose, He created everything with the ability to reproduce. This is why every plant bears within itself the seed of its likeness.

> *"Then God said, 'Let the earth bring forth grass, the herb that yields seed, and the fruit tree that yields fruit according to its kind, whose seed is in itself, on the earth'; and it was so. And the earth brought forth grass, the herb that yields seed according to its kind and the tree that yields fruit, whose seed is in itself according to its kind, And God saw that it was good."*
> *Genesis 1:11&12*

This is God's divine design for multiplication. He actually created each plant with the seed it needs to reproduce its fruit. And remember that we learned in the principles of reaping and sowing that not only will there be seed, but there will be *more* seed than was originally sown. Think about the beauty of that. It would be very difficult for us to stop the natural process of reproduction... many of us have experienced this with weeds that grow in our lawns! Once they begin to grow, it is hard to stop that growth. In fact, I once learned that the best way to get rid of weeds, or bad seed, in your lawn is to plant more good seed. The idea is that the good seed will actually strangle the weeds and overgrow them.

A farmer knows that in the fall comes the provision for spring and that the seed he needs to plant his crop is gathered in the fall. So it is with us. The seed we need for our springtime, our new beginnings, is accumulated through the fruit of our fall. This is why we must harvest and bring in the fruit. Therein lies our seed for multiplication and growth. This goes back to our design to produce and increase. Just like in the natural, His design for our spiritual growth is acquired through spiritual cycles.

STEWARD THE SEED

Every experience you go through has a seed within it; even your "bad" ones. Your job is to learn how to steward that seed for your good and God's glory. You plant that seed to reproduce either bitter fruit or good fruit. I often say that my greatest successes have come out of my greatest failures. This is because God has taught me how to steward every seed and intentionally plant it in His timing, in the right place, thus bearing good fruit. This is where spiritually we have the power to defy the natural law of the seed. This is where repentance is often required.

REPENTANCE

When we recognize that it is because of our own disobedient sowing that we bear bitter fruit, we must acknowledge it and agree with God in our sin. Realize that this is not necessarily always as overt as we think. To sow where God has not called us to sow is sin, and to not sow where God has called us to sow is also sin. Sometimes we recognize this; sometimes it happens out of ignorance. Either way, if you see bitter fruit, it is important to let God examine your "sowing process." Ask Him to show you what seeds you have been sowing, where you have been sowing them, when you have sown them, and why. You must let God search your heart for the motive behind why you do what you do. Often, we think we are sowing out of a pure heart, but when we let the Holy Spirit look, we may find that we are walking in the flesh.

"All the ways of a man are pure in his own eyes, but the Lord weighs the spirit."

Proverbs 16:2

The word *spirit* here is referring to the heart of man, meaning the motives that are within us. He is faithful and loving to reveal the depths of why we do what we do. If we allow this and are willing to be corrected, God will, in His kindness and tenderness, allure us into a place of repentance that leaves no regrets.

"But we know that the judgment of God is according to truth against those who practice such things. And do you think this, O man, you who judge those practicing such things, and doing the same, that you will escape the judgment of God? Or do you despise the riches of His goodness, forbearance, and longsuffering, not knowing that the goodness of God leads you to repentance?"

Romans 2:3&4

"For godly sorrow produces repentances leading to salvation, not to be regretted; but the sorrow of the world produces death."

2 Corinthians 7:10

Repentance offers the opportunity to take seed born of bad fruit and replant it in a place of obedience and water it with His love, shifting the nature of that seed into something good. This is the nature of God. It is His desire to use all things to bring about good in our lives (Romans 8:28). In the Spirit, nothing is wasted. Even what the enemy intends for evil, God will use for good when you surrender to His will.

"But as for you, you meant evil against me; but God meant it for good."

Genesis 50:20

"If we confess our sins, He is faithful and just to forgive us our sins and to cleanse us from all unrighteousness."

1 John 1:9

Repentance breaks the root of the bad seed and replants it in the fertile soil of the Holy Spirit, thus bringing forth good fruit.

This is true not just of seed we have planted, but of seed that has been planted into us generationally. Through the blood of Christ, our power to navigate every seed can break generational curses in our lives. When we come to Jesus, His seed is planted within us and we are grafted into His family tree and with it comes His DNA.

"Whoever has been born of God does not sin, for His seed remains in him; and he cannot sin, because he has been born of God."

1 John 3:9

The seed of Jesus will cause us to bear good fruit, but our job is to tenderly steward that seed by living with obedience. When we do, we will organically reap His fullness no matter our past, failures, or heritage. The spiritual will trump the natural!

"And if some of the branches were broken off, and you, being a wild olive tree, were grafted in among them, and with them became a partaker of the root and fatness of the olive tree."

Romans 11:17

So, even the harvest that produces bad seed can be used for your good and His glory. God is so good and He will stop at nothing to see you and I come into a life of fullness; that is the "fatness of the olive tree."

Isaiah prophesies this same concept in Isaiah 61. He says that there is one who is coming that will not only save us, heal us and deliver us, but will also restore us from generational "baggage."

"And they shall rebuild the old ruins, They shall raise up the former desolations, And they shall repair the ruined cities, The desolations of many generations."

Isaiah 61:4

The Message reads this way:

"They'll rebuild the old ruins, raise a new city out of the wreckage. They'll start over on the ruined cities, take the rubble left behind and make it new."

There is nothing the blood of Jesus cannot redeem. Whether it is the rubble of your own choices, or the rubble of your heritage, God will rebuild something new. Not a seed is wasted in the Kingdom!

Our fall season has much purpose beyond just reaping the fruit. Fall plays a vital part in keeping the rest of the seasons cycling. It is our sustenance in the winter and our seed for spring and our hope during summer! It is when we learn to see each seed that comes out of our *chronos* happenings through the *kairos* lens of God's seasons and cycles that we will gain understanding of the fullness of His fruit.

☙ PRAYER PRACTICE

Father, what a beautiful process You have created in the seed. The DNA of each plant, flower, and creature is held within itself. I thank You for the purposes of the harvest and importance that has in life and in my spiritual growth. I praise You Lord for the beauty of regeneration and the way I have seen it in my own life. Thank You Lord for putting Your seed within me and causing me to bear good fruit...that others may taste and see that You are good! In Jesus' name, Amen.

Chapter 15 Gathering the Harvest

"And it shall be that if you earnestly obey My commandments which I command you today, to love the Lord your God and serve Him with all your heart and with all your soul, then I will give you the rain for your land in its season, the early rain and the latter rain that you may gather in your grain, your new wine, and your oil. And I will send grass in your fields for your livestock, that you may eat and be filled."

Deuteronomy 11:13-15

We have seen in Scripture and learned through creation that it is God's design that we come into seasons of fall, which are seasons of fruit and abundance. That we will indeed come to the place of much "grain, wine, and oil." This is a promise that we can stand on. If that is the case, why is it that many of us never actually experience or "eat of" that abundance? I believe it is because we need to learn how to harvest.

HARVESTING

Consider the definition of harvesting for a moment. I personally like to use the word harvest because I think it encompasses more effectively what it means to reap the fullness of our labors. Think about this, as a farmer, I could plant and sow seed, then be diligent to cultivate and nurture that seed all summer long. Then, into the fall, I would reap fruit. However, if I want to eat of that fruit, I have to harvest it. There is more work to be done! I must get back out into the field and bring the fruit in. Many of us think that we are supposed to just sit back and wait on God to drop fruit into our laps. Of course there are times when God blesses us with that very thing. But more often than not, we have to go harvest the fruit, meaning, go get it! Once we see the fruit of God in our lives, we must be tenacious for it. Personally, I am going to get after it, go get it, and bring it to my table for me to eat! I believe this is what separates believers who sit in the wilderness from those who reap the fullness of the milk and honey of His promises. We cycle through winter, spring, and summer, and see fruit, but never understand the harvesting of fall, thus always planting, but never experiencing abundance.

I am personally in this season. Just this week, I found myself seeking God for answers to increase the financial resources we need to continue caring for the families in our housing program effectively. He reminded me of the harvesting process. I then realized that I have spent many years sowing into our community, cultivating relationships, and establishing our credibility. I see the fruit through much favor with churches, businesses, schools, and the government. As I asked the Lord to turn that favor into financial resources, I heard Him say, "Go get it!" He said it is time to harvest that fruit. I need to go out into the field and bring it in. As such, I have spent much of my week actually going to people whom He has brought to mind and simply asking them to be a monthly donor. These are people that already know us and recognize the value of our services at Crazy8 Ministries. Our credibility is established with them and they are favorable toward us. It has been ridiculous how easy it has been and how quickly these people have responded saying yes. You see, the fruit was there, but I needed to go get it! This is what it means to harvest.

I want to be sure to state that I am not saying we must work for our blessings, because that is not the case. We serve a God of grace who has given us many amazing blessings. One of the most incredible things He has given to us is power and authority. Yet, often we don't utilize that power and we end up waiting on God to do what He has given us the power and authority to do.

I love the story of Moses and the lesson we learn through his rod. The rod is a picture of the power and authority that God handed to Moses to use for signs, miracles, and wonders. He invited Moses to be a part of the manifestation of His works. A good example of Moses not using that power is seen when the Israelites stood in front of the Red Sea crying out to God for help.

"And the Lord said to Moses, "Why do you cry to Me? Tell the children of Israel to go forward. But, lift up your rod, and

stretch out your hand over the sea and divide it. And the children of Israel shall go on dry ground through the midst of the sea."

Exodus 14:15&16

God is in a sense saying, "Why are you calling on Me to do what I have given you the power to do?" What a lesson we can learn from this. I see so often people who sit back wondering why God isn't just dropping healing, deliverance, and blessings into their laps, when God is saying, "I have invited you to partake in My work. Now use the resources and tools that I have given and go forward in power and authority to part those waters. Go get your promise!"

ADD THE WORK TO THE WORD

Again, I want to be careful not to focus on works, but we do need to recognize that God invites us to work with Him. I once spoke at a church on how we must add action to His Word to reap the promise. In other words, His Word + a work = the promise. There are so many examples of this in Scripture.

One of my favorite examples is of Hannah in 1 Samuel 1. She was barren and went to the temple to pray and ask God for a child. Eli the priest told her that she would bear a child, thus receiving a Word from God. It is important to note what happened next.

"So the woman went her way and ate, and her face was no longer sad. Then they rose early in the morning and worshiped before the Lord, and returned and came to their house at Ramah. And Elkanah knew Hannah his wife, and the Lord remembered her."

1 Samuel 1:18&19

Hannah received the Word with faith, and then added to it the action of intimacy with her husband. In other words, His Word plus her action literally birthed the promise.

Other examples like, Naaman who received the Word of healing, but needed to go and wash in order for that healing to manifest. In fact, he even asked why the prophet couldn't just wave his hand over him for healing. Can God do that? Of course He can,

He is God, but more often than not, He invites us to be a part of our healing process. The man with the crippled hand was told to "stretch out his hand." The lame man was told to "pick up his mat." You see the actions here? God typically sends us forth with action items. It is through these actions that our promises manifest. We can't just look at the fruit; we have to go get it!

Listen, we are not just saved to get to heaven, it is not just about eternity. You have a divine assignment here on earth. You and I are the intersection between the spiritual and natural. Kairos happenings manifest through our chronos events. We are here to cause earth to look a little more like heaven.

"Your kingdom come. Your will be done on earth as it is in heaven."

Matthew 6:10

It was through the disciples that the multitude was fed. Remember? Jesus said, "You give them something to eat" (Mark 6:37). He told them that the multitude would be fed, thus giving them a Word, but then invited them to take part in the manifestation of the miracle. On faith, the disciples added the action of dispersing the food, which mind you was only five loaves and two fish when they started.

"And when He had taken the fives loaves and the two fish, He looked up to heaven, blessed and broke the loaves, and gave them to His disciples to set before them."

Mark 6:41

It wasn't until the disciples began to function on faith that the miracle manifested. Action was needed to collide the provision of heaven with the needs on earth, and the disciples were the vessel through which that miracle poured out. They were the intersection between the spiritual and the natural. They were not the source of the miracle, but they were indeed a part of the miracle. Could God have just dropped food from the sky? Yes! Could Jesus have dispersed the food, or multiplied it beforehand? Yes! Instead, God was teaching the disciples how to practice the power and authority they had to cause a supernatural shift in this world.

This reflects back to our struggle against self-pity and victimization. That mindset will prevent you from stepping in to the power that God has given us to cause a change in our own life. We have more power than we think. Remember the man at the Pool of Bethesda in John 5? When Jesus asked, "Do you want to be made well?" The man began to give all these reasons why he wasn't able to be healed and well. He gave excuses! Jesus dismissed that sad spirit of self-pity and instead gave a call to action saying, "Rise, take up your bed and walk." I wonder what would have happened if the lame man would have just sat back and not added the action to the word of God? This is a picture of where I feel many believers are. We are crippled, lame, broken, bitter, depressed, in lack, etc. and instead of rising up and walking, or raising our rod of power and authority, we settle on our mats in the wilderness, living in lack and shaking our fists at God for not delivering us into our promises.

❧ PRAYER PRACTICE

Lord, I thank You for inviting me to partner with you in Your work. I recognize Lord that I must listen for Your action items and do what You say. I pray that You open my eyes to see the tools that You have given me and that you give me the wisdom to know how to use them. I pray that I am not found waiting on You when it is actually that You are waiting on me. May I be a doer of Your Word and may I remember that it is when we function on faith that signs follow. In Jesus' name, Amen.

APPROPRIATING THE SPOILS

There are blessings that come with your salvation beyond just your eternal well-being. To be reconciled with God means to be brought back together with God, as well as having your blessings restored. There is an inheritance that comes with our salvation, which I call the spoils of the cross. Think about all the battles that the Israelites won where they did not just gain the victory, but they collected spoils. Jehoshaphat in 2 Chronicles 20 is a great example of this. They gained a victory that left them with three days' worth of spoil to collect.

> *"When Jehoshaphat and his people came to take away their spoil, they found among them an abundance of valuables on the dead bodies, and precious jewelry, which they stripped off for themselves, more than they could carry away; and they were three days gathering the spoil because there was so much."*
>
> *2 Chronicles 20:25*

The spoil was there, but they had to collect it. They appropriated the spoil, which means, "to take something for one's own use typically without the owner's permission." To take that definition and transfer it to appropriate the spoils of the cross means we know the rights we have been given and the inheritance that we received through the blood of Jesus and we make it our own. Because the Israelites had won the battle, the spoil was theirs to take; they were given the right to it, or authority over it. Jesus has won the victory for us and with that victory comes a spoil that we are given the right or authority to collect every day of our lives. Many of us have not learned to collect the spoil, or harvest the fruit of our falls. This is why we miss out on feasting on His fullness; we aren't harvesting the fruit.

WHAT IS DUE YOU

I am shocked how many believers think they are reaping the fullness of life when they have settled in the wilderness. They don't realize that there is always more freedom and blessings to be had; blessings that we have the authority to walk in with confidence. The authority that we carry because of His name gives us the victory over Satan and his thieving ways in our lives. Remember, Satan has the same power that we have, but he has no authority. God gave dominion to man, not Satan. It is Satan's goal to get us to hand our authority over to him. When we do so, we allow defeat, depression, anger, pride, fear, addiction, bitterness, etc. to gain dominion or authority over us.

"The thief does not come except to steal, and to kill, and to destroy. I have come that they may have life, and that they may have it more abundantly."

John 10:10

That word *abundant* means "excessive, overflowing, surplus, over and above, more than enough." That is a pretty powerful word. Jesus said He came that we would have life *more* abundantly. I don't know about you, but I am thinking there is more to be had... and I want the overflow and excessive blessings of God in my life.

One of our first challenges as counselors is getting our clients to realize that they are missing out on what God wants to give them. Getting them to realize what is due them because of the work of the cross and who they are in Christ. I mean, we are children of the Most High God and that comes with a mighty inheritance of a more abundant life. God has put unction in us by the Holy Spirit to pursue this life; to be tenacious for it.

"I found it necessary to write to you exhorting you to contend earnestly for the faith which was once for all delivered to the saints."

Jude 3

The word *contend* means "struggle to surmount or engage in a competition or campaign in order to win or achieve." That's rich! God has called us to earnestly engage in the battle for the purpose of achieving and winning the fullness of our salvation. Know the rights you have as a child of God and fight for them!

When you have been faithful through each of the spiritual seasons and you come to a place where you see fruit, go after it; harvest that fruit and bring it to your table. Wrestle for it like Jacob did in the wilderness when he knew the land where he was going into was his promise. It was his inheritance and he had the rights to it. In his wrestling he contended with God and held Him to His promise stating, "I am not letting you go until you bless me." Now that's tenacity. Live boldly and expect God to do big things and to bless you more abundantly.

℮ PRAYER PRACTICE

Father, I thank You for the authority that You have given me to walk in your power and collect my inheritance. I refuse to give my authority over to the devil and let him keep me from the overflow You have in mind for me. I loosen the unction that You have placed within me to fight and earnestly contend for all that you settled once and for all on the cross. I recognize that Your death was not just to save me eternally, but it was also to bless me here on earth. I receive that Truth and I won't stop until I see it on my table. In Jesus' name, Amen.

16 Missing Harvest Time

O ne of the saddest chapters in the Scriptures is Numbers 13. The irony is that it had the potential to actually be a moment of great victory for the Israelites. It was the moment they had been waiting for... the entry into their promise. After a tumultuous escape from the hands of their captors, and a walk of faith through the wilderness, the fruit of what they had been striving for was right in front of their eyes... literally! Moses had sent twelve spies to check the land out and see what it was like.

> "...see what the land is like; whether the people who dwell in it are strong or weak, few or many; whether the land they dwell in is good or bad; whether the cities they inhabit are like camps or strongholds; whether the land is rich or poor; and whether there are forests there or not. Be of good courage. AND BRING SOME OF THE FRUIT OF THE LAND." Now the time was the season of the first ripe grapes."
>
> Numbers 13:18-20
> (emphasis mine)

Moses knew it was the season for fruit and he instructed them to bring some back, which they did.

> "Then they came to the Valley of Eshcol, and there cut down a branch with one cluster of grapes...they also brought some of the pomegranates and figs...they brought back word to them and to all the congregation, and showed them the fruit of the land. Then they told him, and said: 'We went to the land where you sent us. It truly flows with milk and honey, and this is its fruit.'"
>
> Numbers 13:23, 26&27

The fruit was there! The provision and blessing of God was

not in question. God had been faithful and surely had brought them to their season of abundance, the Promised Land, just as He had said. The evidence was tangible and right before their eyes, however, they had to go get it. The only things in question here were the hearts of the Israelites. Remember, we have to appropriate the goods of God, meaning to take something for our own use. That fruit was not going to come to them, they had to go claim it and take possession of it.

> *"Then Caleb quieted the people before Moses, and said, "Let us go up at once and take possession, for we are well able to overcome it."*
>
> *Numbers 13:30*

Caleb exhorted the Israelites to go get their inheritance. He was in a sense saying, "Here's the fruit, now it's time to harvest it!" God had given them a Word, and with it, evidence, and now there was a call to action. Through the addition of their action, the promise would manifest and become reality.

Unfortunately, most of us know what happened instead. Despite the evidence and the reminder of God's promise, they did not go get their inheritance. As a result, they wandered in the wilderness for another forty years. Now, let it be said that although God's presence never left them, and He provided for them and loved them in the wilderness, they settled for less than what God had in mind for them. I wonder how many of us have done the same. We miss out on milk and honey and settle in a "land of lack" because we didn't harvest the fruit. Like the Israelites, God still is with us, and He still provides for us and loves us, yet, we do not reap the fullness of what God intends for us in this life.

HARVEST BARRIERS

What keeps us from getting after our fruit and harvesting it? Let's look a bit closer at Numbers 13 for the answer, so we learn and grow. We have already discussed most of these concepts, but I cannot help but show you confirmation through the Word.

"But the men who had gone up with him said, 'We are not able to go up against the people, for they are stronger than we.' And they gave the children of Israel a bad report of the land which they had spied out, saying, 'The land through which we have gone as spies is a land that devours its inhabitants, and all the people whom we saw in it are men of great stature. 'There we saw the giants (the descendants of Anak came from the giants); and we were like grasshoppers in our own sight, and so we were in their sight.'"

Numbers 13:32&33

We see here that the Israelites were in doubt. They questioned their ability to overtake the people who currently possessed their land. Doubt comes from a lack of perspective. When our focus shifts away from God and onto the world, we will waver in our faith.

THE PLUMB LINE

Comparing our abilities to what we see in the world, instead of to what God says, triggers a lack of faith and opens the door to doubt. The world and the people in it are not your measuring stick. God is!

In Amos chapter 7, Amos has an encounter in which he sees God holding a plumb line. A plumb line is a cord weighted with lead that is used to ensure that a structure is built vertically. It establishes the integrity of the building. Symbolically it represents the fact that God Himself sets the standard by which we build and it is by His standard that our integrity is established. He used the vision of the plumb line to show that it is God who measures what is straight and true. He is the One to let us know whether or not we are building a "straight" path that is in accordance to His standard. God has measured us by the blood of Jesus, but the world has a totally different way of measuring us.

IDENTITY

Our standard of measure is ultimately where we will find our identity. The world continually measures us based on education, career, by our size and how we look, even by the car we drive. This process starts the day we are born, and we must not buy into it. The world's way of defining us will steal our identity in Christ. Look at how the Israelites literally allowed the physical measurement of the world to define their identity.

> "...and we were like grasshoppers in our own sight, and so we were in their sight."
>
> *Numbers 13:33*

They were not grasshoppers; they were children of God! But, in their wanderings, they lost sight of their identity in God.

In my line of work, I often see people fall prey to the world's way of defining them. Just as often, I see people fall prey to their own feelings and emotions too, which is just as devastating. Our emotions and thoughts will threaten to define us and navigate our lives. We must learn to live according to who we are, not how we feel or what we think. I don't always *feel* victorious, and I certainly don't always see victory in my life. However, according to God's Word, I am a conqueror and I am led about in a triumphant procession in Jesus Christ. That is the truth of who I am and what makes me step out and advance in the midst of natural impossibility. The thoughts and feelings of the Israelites did not just cause them defeat, it kept them from even stepping out and trying. They never even got out onto the field to play the game! They sat on the sidelines shaking in their shoes.

PRAYER PRACTICE

God, I am reminded that You are the plumb line by which the standard for my life is set. I agree that I am not who the world says I am, I agree that I am not what I feel, I agree that I am not what my natural mind says, and I am not the summation of my failures or my successes. I am who You say that I am... and I look like You because I am Your child. I walk in love, I am patient, I am confident, and I am highly favored by You. I am the apple of Your eye! With confidence in the rights that I have as Your

child, I enter into Your throne room daily and I come out running into the battlefield. Thank You for empowering me with Your truths and for filling me with courage to fight! In Your Holy Name I pray, Amen.

Things and people in this world will often seem so big, that they cannot be overcome. Truthfully, many times in the natural world, they can't. However, God is a supernatural God so it is not unlike Him to call us to overthrow places and circumstances and people that are much bigger than we can handle in our own strength and resources. God is in the business of leading His people to a place of natural impossibility. Remember how He cut Gideon's army down from thirty-two thousand men to three hundred? Or how Simon Peter's fishing net broke in Luke chapter 5? Or how there were only two fish and five loaves, but a multitude of people? In every case, God came through and no man could boast. It was only because of God! In each of these cases, the people also came to understand more of their potential. They learned the fullness of who they were and what they could accomplish as children of God.

This is how God brings us into our true identity, and we must not forget it! When we meditate on God and His bigness and His power and His love, everything else seems so pitiful and will fade away. Remembering your position in the kingdom and the truth that you are His child will ward off doubt and fear that will cloud your identity and steal what is rightfully yours.

We forget who we are and what is due us. We are children of the Most High God and with that title comes God's inheritance. The Israelites were unable to move forward on faith because they forgot who they were and therefore, what was rightfully theirs as the children of God. Their loss of identity kept them from even entering into battle; they wouldn't even get on the playing field. Not to sound cliché, but to know *who* we are, we must remember *whose* we are. This basic remembrance is what separated David from Saul's Army. David was mindful that they were children of God, and therefore the land that was guarded by Goliath was theirs to take. Tenacity rose up in him that caused him to stand up, not only to the enemy, but to his own brethren who mocked his confidence. Much like the Israelites in Numbers, David's obstacle was bigger and stronger, and no doubt he looked like a grasshopper compared to Goliath. However, his focus on God and his confidence in his position with God caused the unction that drove him to overthrow that barrier.

One of the things that saddens me is seeing how we, as the children of God, look more like Saul's army than we look like David. Like the soldiers, we are dressed in the armor of God, but we sit on the sidelines, complaining about our defeat. David was a warrior, and warriors fearlessly advance with passion for what is right. They stand and fight for what they know to be true and they are willing to fight to the death. They would rather die than settle in defeat. Here are some questions to ask yourself. Are you a warrior who's ready and willing to take the field? Are you willing to take a stand for what you know is due you? Will you advance even when your own brethren don't support you?

As believers we must know the fullness of what God wants to give us. Many of us have never moved beyond our eternal salvation to recognize the blessings and riches of our inheritance that is due us while we are still on earth. I truly believe that no matter how much I have had of God and His love and His blessings, there is always more. He is a God of increase and He is ever growing us. It delights Him to bless us. The fact that He "lavishes" us with His love and covers us with kisses (see the story of the prodigal son) demonstrates that He is a Father who loves to spoil His children with good things.

> *"Behold what manner of love the Father has bestowed on us, that we should be called children of God!"*
>
> *1 John 3:1*

One of my favorite songs right now is called "No Longer Slaves" by Bethel. The chorus is simply two lines, yet encompass a powerful Truth.

> *"I'm no longer a slave to fear, I am a child of God."*

Look at the antidote that is given for the liberation of fear: To declare that you are a child of God. The song is a reminder that to walk enslaved in fear is to forget that you are His child. I had the privilege of seeing this song performed live and I will never forget it. It wasn't just the lyrics that were powerful, it was the resounding declaration of those who were singing it. Their faith in this truth resonated through the air, permeating my skin and piercing my soul. I don't know how anyone could have left enslaved to fear after the way His law of love was enforced that night!

℮ PRAYER PRACTICE

> *Father, I thank You that You remind me daily of who I am, that I am a child of God. I thank You that You do not measure me the way the world does, but when You look at me You see who I really am in the Spirit. I thank You that You don't count my failures or my successes and You don't put a letter grade on my day. You are not like the world, and I am not who the world says I am. I am Your child. I agree that my fullness is beyond what I could ever imagine and that You have great things in mind for me. I anticipate and expect that You will continue to expand my horizons and deepen my walk. And I expect that You will increase my life and bring me into more fruit and more productivity in all things. I praise You Father in the name of Jesus, Amen.*

Although it would be correct to say that the Israelites struggled with fear, it would only be addressing the symptom. Fear is the outcome. The root was that they forgot who they were. They allowed the world to measure them, thus defining them as less than what was true. Their false identity stole their unction to harvest what was rightfully due them… The Promised Land. They saw the fruit they had been waiting for, but never got to reap it.

17 Another Harvest Season

U nlike Numbers 13, the book of Joshua is one of victory. It is almost like the antithesis of Numbers 13. Joshua is the book in which we see that God redeems the Israelites by bringing them back around to the Promised Land once again and giving them yet another chance to step into fullness.

We have already spent some time looking at Joshua 1, when Joshua steps into his new position, so let's fast forward to chapter 8. It is forty years after what took place in Numbers 13 and they have come to the same land. Only this time, they chose to harvest. They got after it and claimed what was theirs! We see here that their mindset is completely different and they know they must advance. They recognize who they are and what is theirs.

> *"Now the Lord said to Joshua: "Do not be afraid, do not be dismayed, take all the people of war with you, and arise, go up to Ai. See, I have given in to your hand the king of Ai, his people, his city, and his land."*
>
> *Joshua 8:1*

Funny that God says almost the same thing that He had spoken to them forty years prior in Numbers 13. There is the exact same call to action (word) being given and the same promise as well. This time, the Israelites move in faith and not fear. Our promise is birthed out of the action that we add to the Word. This is why they never reaped the fruit in Numbers 13. They were indeed given a promise from God, but they did not add to it the work of harvesting the fruit and missed out on what was due them; they missed out on the milk and honey.

Let's note all that the Israelites had to overcome in order to go forth in action on faith.

FEAR/DISMAY

God starts by exhorting Joshua not to give in to fear or dismay. God knows the natural heart of man better than we do, and He is wise to address its inclinations before we know we need it. He realizes that this will be a time where they will once again face the challenge of fear and dismay. The Bible does not tell us that walking in victory is the absence of such challenges, but rather walking in victory is reaping fruit despite those challenges. This is why David says in Psalm 23:5 that He prepares a table before us in the presence of our enemies. David knew full well that we will continually have "face-offs" with our enemies, but when we trust in God, we can be "fat and happy" and triumphant even in those moments. I love that God adds the word "dismayed" to fear. The word *dismayed* in the Hebrew language means to "be shattered, broken, or abolished." *To abolish* means to "put an end to or to exterminate." Doesn't this sound just like the motive of the enemy? He wants nothing more than to exterminate the children of God and bring us to an end, and he does this by fear and intimidation. God gives the remedy for this in His statement, "Arise."

ARISE

The word *arise* in Hebrew encompasses a lot more than just getting up or standing up, although there is power in that as well. Sometimes, when we wake up in the morning and the weight of life sits on our chest and in our minds, we would do well to remember the power of hearing Him say, "Arise," and then following that word with the action of simply getting up! Beyond that, the word includes the idea of "coming onto the scene and being established." There is a sense of coming into oneself. God is saying, "Step into your identity and take what is yours!" There is power in remembering that we are God's children and that He loves us. That resolution will drive out all fear.

> *"There is no fear in love; but perfect love casts out fear, because fear involves torment. But he who fears has not been made perfect in love."*
>
> *1 John 4:18*

Our identity begins in believing that we are loved perfectly by God. When we can come to that place and walk in it confidently, we will arise to new levels and step into new things. We will be coming on to the scene and causing shifts and changes that we never thought possible. Doing things like starting ministries, housing the homeless, traveling the country, and ministering healing in Wal-Mart. And we will be confident in the promises of God, the fruit that is due us, and our ability to harvest the fruit.

> *"And you shall do to Ai and its king as you did to Jericho and its king. Only its spoil and its cattle you shall take as booty for yourselves."*
>
> *Joshua 8:2*

THE BOOTY OF GOD

I love this word. Here is a biblical truth: Obedience brings in the booty. OK, cheesy, I know, but I bet you will remember it. Booty is the take away; it is what you walk away with after the battle; it is your reward. We talked earlier about the spoils of God. God uses every battle for good in our lives. There is *always* a take away that you can learn and grow from. Watch and expect the booty or the reward of God. Even when you feel you have lost a battle, there is a take-away.

The Word promises that when you walk in the ways of God, blessings will come to you. I absolutely love Deuteronomy 28. It is such an overwhelming picture of how much God wants to bless. It starts by encouraging us to "diligently" obey the voice of God and the blessings of God will then be released. And the blessings are so much that they will "overtake you."

> *"And all these blessings shall come upon you and overtake you, because you obey the voice of the Lord your God."*
>
> *Deuteronomy 28:2*

That statement is followed up by multiple statements that start with the phrase, "You shall." You shall is not a suggestion, it is a promise. Now I know that many of you, including myself right now, are thinking, *"Why does this not seem to be true for me?"* Remember,

God's ways are different than ours. It is His timing, His work, and His plan. Our job is to believe and obey...and expect! I am not suggesting that you be presumptuous, but I am suggesting that if God says you shall take booty, then you can and should expect that you will take booty!

IF-THEN

Here is a summary so far of Joshua 8 in my words: "You have a choice: You can fear and be dismayed, or you can remember who you are and the rights you have. **If** you choose to stand and be established in your identity, and arise, **then** you will reap the reward of God."

I love when I see such clear "if-then" statements in Scripture. It reminds me of the choice I have and the promises I can stand on. Just hearing and even believing that if-then statement was not enough. Joshua had to add action to it!

"So Joshua arose, and all the people of war, to go up against Ai."
Joshua 8:3

DOING THE WORD

This whole verse is good, but I think the phrase, "So Joshua arose," is so powerful! Just as God said, so Joshua did! God said, "Arise," and Joshua arose. It is simple, yet, so powerful. Faith is demonstrated through action.

Consider this: When God gave Noah a directive, his faith was seen daily in that he diligently worked on building the Ark. Faith is seen not heard.

"For the kingdom of God is not in word, but in power."
1 Corinthians 4:20

Jesus Christ *positions* us for the work of the kingdom, but the Holy Spirit *empowers* us for the work of the kingdom. When we stand confidently in our position (our identity), we recognize not just our power, but our right to walk in that power. Power is displayed and not just talked about. I know a lot of believers who know what Scriptures says, but have yet to execute it. This lack of action will keep you from the promises of God, just as it kept the Israelites in Numbers 13 from the Promised Land.

Joshua's belief and obedience then led others into the path of victory as well. He repeated the promise of God with confidence through action as well as in word. He commands with boldness the strategy of the battle to his men and ends with the promise spoken with resounding confidence in verses 7&8.

> *"Then you shall rise from the ambush and seize the city, for the Lord your God will deliver it into your hand. And it will be, when you have taken the city, that you shall set the city on fire. According to the commandment of the Lord you shall do. See, I have commanded you."*

Notice that Joshua reminds them that God is *their* God, thus encouraging them by reminding them of who they are. It is because of that truth that they shall seize the city, meaning take possession of it. But, that land was not going to just fall into their lap; they had to go get it. Taking possession means go harvest the fruit!

PRAYER PRACTICE

> *Lord, I am reminded of who I am right in this moment and I meditate on the truth that I am a child of God and with that comes a rightful inheritance. I am expecting that in this day, as I walk in who I am and am not swayed by the definitions of the world, that I will reap the fruit of Your Spirit that is within me. I loosen You to bless me more fully and I break off any hindrances that would keep me from the booty of Your kingdom. In Jesus' name, Amen.*

WHAT YOU MUST KNOW

Now, I could stop this chapter here and say that my point is made, but I can't. I am compelled to go on and share with you more principles that we need to know when harvesting the fruit of God.

THE EASE OF GOD

"So they (the people of Ai) left the city open and pursued Israel."
Joshua 8:17

Because of Joshua's strategy that was given to him through the wisdom of the Lord, the people of Ai were "tricked" into leaving their city wide open and unguarded. For the details, read the whole chapter, but for the sake of time, let me jump to the point. It is not unlike God to go before us and "clear the path" to victory. Hear me when I say that to obey is often not easy and it doesn't always feel good either. We deceive ourselves to say otherwise. However, although obedience is often hard, the reward of that obedience often comes easy. Our obedience releases His blessings so the outcome of our obedience feels great and is automatic in its return. We see that in this passage. The fight was not actually even with the enemy, it was within the Israelites' own minds...would they or would they not believe God and obey in faith? This is where they lost in Numbers 13.

When we follow God's path on faith, we can trust that He is going before us clearing the path.

"The breaker [the Messiah, who opens the way] shall go up before them [liberating them]. They will break out, pass through the gate and go out; So their King goes on before them, The Lord at their head."
Micah 2:13
Amplified Version

I have heard God referred to as the Breaker Anointing that is released when we obey. There are so many passages in the Scriptures that talk about the path that He provides and leads us on. He makes our paths straight and prepares the way for easy entrance into the will He has for us. Without our action, this will be nothing but a promise that we never come into.

"For My yoke is easy and My burden is light."
Matthew 11:30

There is a certain ease in walking with God. Now, this word "easy" does not mean what we think nor does it translate the way we would define it. It actually denotes the idea of being "useful, pleasant, suitable or fitting." It also encompasses the word *kindly*, meaning it is kind. This does not always mean it feels good, but rather it fits rightly. When we are yoked to God and His Word, we will find ourselves just walking into freedom, just as they did here in Joshua 8. The enemy will be removed and utterly destroyed. Being yoked to God, however, requires surrender and obedience; a willingness to go right when He turns right and left when He turns left. This is how two oxen yoked together function. They become as one in the way they move. To fight against the yoke is exhausting to the ox and counterproductive to why he is yoked in the first place.

This is what it is like for us as children of God to fight against the will of God, which is found in His Word. God likened this action to that of kicking against the goads (Acts 9:5). A goad is a pointed stick that was used to poke an ox to encourage him in the right direction. To kick against that would only bring about pain. Boy, can I relate to that!

PERSEVERE IN OBEDIENCE

I want to talk to you a moment about persevering in obedience. There is a difference between obeying and persevering in obedience. God has taught me this over and over as I have grown in Him. There are times when God calls us to obey, and it is a single action. There are even more times in life when we have to walk in obedience. It is a constant choice to make over and over again. This can be challenging and wearisome, especially if you are in the throes of trying circumstances and emotions.

In Mark chapter 5, the woman with the issue of blood set her mind on her healing before she touched the edge of Jesus' cloak saying, "If only I may touch His clothes, I shall be made well" (verse 28). In Daniel chapter 1, Daniel set his mind that he would not defy himself with the king's food before he faced the chief of the eunuchs. Verse 8 says, "He purposed in his heart." The word, *purpose* in Hebrew means to "put, place, set, appoint, direct, ordain, or establish." The word *heart* in Hebrew encompasses the mind and the will, meaning the inner man, or soul. So to purpose in your heart means to make up your mind and establish your choice, but the key is to do so beforehand.

The word *perseverance* means to "be steadfast in doing something despite difficulty or delay in achieving success." When Jesus set His face toward Jerusalem in Luke 9:51, He was purposed in His heart and established in His mind. He knew what God's will was and He was unwilling to sway from that will. The same was true for Daniel and the woman with the issue of blood. When we are convinced of God's Word (His promise) to us, we should predetermine that we will not stop pressing into that word until we see it come to pass.

GOD'S GRACE

God is so gracious in His redemptive nature. Just as He wanted for the Israelites, He so desperately wants us to reap fullness that He will bring us back around season after season to harvest the fruit of fall. Although the Israelites missed the harvest the first time around, God brought them back and gave them a second chance. He is a God of redemption, which I like to say means He is a God of "re-dos." O what a merciful God we serve who refines us and teaches us how to harvest and master every season of fall.

PRAYER PRACTICE

God, I praise You that You are tenacious for me to come into the fullness of my salvation; that You never give up on me and that You predetermined my destiny before I even knew anything about You. You have set for me a course and even when I jump course, You bring me back around to it. Thank You Father for loving me so much and wanting more for me in this life as well as for eternity. You have set for me an example of perseverance just by the way You love me. I release that same spirit within me that I will walk with tenacity and be steadfast in all that I do. In the mighty name of Jesus I pray, Amen!

Conclusion
The Spiral Staircase

Many people compare our walk with God to that of climbing mountains and descending into valleys, or having ups and downs. But I like to think of my walk with God like climbing a spiral staircase. A spiral staircase is different from a regular staircase. Instead of climbing straight up, you cycle up. There is a process of circling around and around when you climb a spiral staircase. And as you climb, you continually circle back around to what feels like the same spot over and over. The difference is that each time, you are actually at a higher level.

Life is much like that. We cycle around and around through the seasons... naturally and spiritually. In the natural, we are able to see that although I have come "back around" to yet another season, I am a year older and I have grown. Unfortunately, we don't often see it the same way as we cycle spiritually. Much like the spiral staircase, when we circle around it can feel like we are in the same spot and progress has not been made. Sometimes we face the same challenges over and over, or contend with the same wound over and over, or encounter the same person over and over. The devil would have us think that we have not grown or progressed in areas of our lives. In looking at how a spiral staircase works, we know that is not true. Just like in the natural, cycling through spiritual seasons is for the purpose of bringing about increase and multiplication in our lives. The challenge is within us to look at it that way! God, in His lovingkindness, is not willing that we would be left lacking or immature. He is ever bringing you into fullness and potential by cycling you through seasons. It is not His desire that you would just survive your seasons, it is His desire that you master them.

"My brethren, count it all joy when you fall into various trials, knowing that the testing of your faith produces patience. But let patience have its perfect work, that you may be perfect and

complete, lacking nothing."

James 1:2&3

I love the writings of Paul in Philippians. In chapter 3, he expresses that he realizes that although he is not perfected, his goal is to press on and into the potential of his perfection in Christ.

"Not that I have already attained, or am already perfected; but I press on, that I may lay hold of that for which Christ Jesus has also laid hold of me. Brethren, I do not count myself to have apprehended; but one thing I do, forgetting those things which are behind and reaching forward to those things which are ahead, I press toward the goal for the prize of the upward call of God in Christ Jesus."

Philippians 3:12-14

His forward thinking is established by his confidence that God is ever-perfecting him. There is no claim to be perfect, but rather a claim to persevere towards grabbing a hold of all that God has for him. Paul understands that there is a cycle spiraling him upward toward a higher call, and that is his hope.

Like Paul, watching for God and knowing His heart is to use every season for our good will fill us with unction for life. We will not fear the seasons, nor will we beg for them to be over. We will learn to rest in the midst of them all.

Winter, a time of dryness or where we see no life; Spring, a time of new beginnings where we are plunging into the great unknown; Summer, a time of busyness where we struggle to be consistent in our intimacy with God; Fall, a time to harvest and go get the fruit of our labor. No matter the season, having a *kairos* mentality will keep you focused on God and expecting your good and His glory. Although God created chronological time, there is a bigger picture and a bigger happening always going on.

"If then you were raised with Christ, seek those things which are above, where Christ is, sitting at the right hand of God. Set your mind on things above, not on things on the earth."

Colossians 3:1&2

The word *mind* here comes from the Greek word *phroneo*, which encompasses the affections of the heart as well as the exercise of the mind. It means to have understanding and be wise. To set your mind here means you are intentional to direct your thinking and feelings on things <u>not</u> of this world. It means that you direct your thoughts upon the *kairos* happenings and watch for the hand of God in all things.

Listen to the resolve that Paul comes to because of his practice of dwelling upon spiritual time and the knowledge of how God is continually working.

> *"Not that I speak in regard to need, for I have learned in whatever state I am, to be content; I know how to be abased, and I know how to abound. Everywhere and in all things I have learned both to be full and to be hungry, both to abound and to suffer need. I can do all things through Christ who strengthens me."*
>
> *Philippians 3:10-13*

Paul is confident that whether he is in lack or in plenty, in winter or in fall, he is able to thrive. But notice he says this is something that he had to learn. In other words, he had to practice setting his mind, not upon his *chronos* circumstances, but rather upon the *kairos* happenings within those circumstances. This is how Paul mastered his seasons.

I fully believe with all my heart that it is God's desire for you and me to walk as Paul did; set upon things above. Know that through every season God is spiraling you upward to the higher calling that is found only in Him. Resolve that merely surviving each season is no longer an option, but mastery is the goal. This mindset will cause you to master the seasons of your life.

About Crazy8 Ministries

Mission: A ministry compelled by the love of Christ to reach and come alongside others and bring healing to the body, soul, and spirit; offering wholeness in yesterday, providing help in today, for a victorious walk in tomorrow.

Crazy8 Ministries was founded in 2011 and started as a conference ministry where founder, Lisa Schwarz, designed and developed conferences and travelled around the United States preaching and teaching the gospel in many arenas. It was her desire to offer more than just a "weekend experience." With people contacting her in need of further ministry, the ministry evolved into what is now the Crazy8 Ministries facility, located on five acres in Joshua, TX. Because each person is at a different place in the healing process of living out the fullness of the gospel, there are several different arms of the ministry. Each arm helps to accomplish the mission through its own unique focus and partner together with one heart and one mind for one purpose: to meet the needs of each person that is served. The goal is to bring those served into the wholeness of Jesus Christ and move them into a place of thriving, body, soul, and spirit.

The Welcome Home Ministry (WHM) is a long term home for women and their children who are in a "sick circumstance" and offer the hope, help and freedom of Jesus Christ in a practical way through a loving, secure, multi-family home. The WHM is an 18-24 month restorative program that is designed to come alongside to provide emotional, spiritual, and physical help in their today, meeting them right where they are.

The Biblical Counseling/Discipleship Ministry (BCDM) focuses on ministering to those who suffer from "sick thinking or sick emotions" through one-on-one free counseling and discipleship as well as group opportunities. The BCDM comes alongside others in order to instill hope, healing, and life transformation through the power of the Holy Spirit and the Word of God, so they may live victoriously in Jesus Christ.

The Outreach Ministry focuses on serving and providing opportunities within our community in order to build relationships and touch others with the love of Christ and the transforming power of the gospel; working toward city transformation by promoting unity and oneness of heart, to proclaim that we are a city of one King.

Crazy8 Ministries founded the City on a Hill Tent Festival held in Burleson, TX. This annual event is a day of free family fun that spotlights the collaboration of services & opportunities working together as the body of Christ in order to transform their community into a 'City on a Hill'. It has grown to serve over 5,000 patrons each year.

To learn more about Crazy8 Ministries, visit www.crazy8ministries.com.

Mission: Enforcing purpose by equipping individuals and empowering lives.

"When our dreams are stirred up and given wings, we are inspired to reach our full potential. I desire to empower people by equipping them with practical skills, encouraging action, and enforcing truth to achieve their purpose" – Lisa Schwarz

SPEAKING SERVICES

Lisa is a national speaker, sought after by groups of all kinds. Her passion is to discern the purpose of her audience, exposing it and releasing it into hearts and minds. Lisa has experience with keynote speaking, as well as conference design and development.

WORKSHOPS AND TRAINING

Lisa is a powerful workshop and training seminar leader. She is gifted in teaching others how to gain the tools that will empower their lives to grow toward excellence and explore all their possibilities. She has years of experience in developing workshops and trainings for all types of groups and incorporates practical hands-on application exercises in order to attain the desired goal.

CONSULTING AND COACHING SERVICES

Bringing dreams to life often takes one-on-one coaching, an area where Lisa excels. Whether it is coming alongside others with training or guiding them into a deeper empowerment of their purpose, she has worked with a wide variety of people and is comfortable in any environment. With a vast background as well as her own training,

Lisa has the experience and expertise to help you turn your dreams into action.

PUBLISHINGS
Discipleship: From Information to Execution

 Learning to follow Jesus is a lifelong process. We are called to be disciples and also called to make disciples. So often today we are clueless on how to do either. Lisa shares the process from her own life: her experience of being discipled and the many believers she has personally discipled. However, in this book, Lisa goes beyond her own experience. She shares the biblical model and vision as well as practical help and guidance on how we, too, can build discipleship into our own lives.

Lisa shares how we can take what we learn and bring it to action in our lives and in the lives of those we seek to encourage in their faith.

> "*Discipleship: From Information to Execution is a meaty manual for leading Christians toward their full potential, as Jesus commanded us to do. If you have tried the traditional methods and felt unsatisfied with the results, pick up a copy of this book and start on a new path. You will be gratified at the practical way to "show, don't tell.""*

To connect with Lisa, visit
www.Lisa-Schwarz.com

About the Cover Art

I was blessed to meet Alison, the artist who drew the image for the front cover, while I was ministering in Cincinnati. The Lord revealed to me a gift for prophetic art within her. Throughout the week, I saw this gift unravel as she sketched things for people I was ministering to. They were not just beautiful, but they were encouraging and relevant to the recipient.

When the time came to design the cover for this book, I knew I wanted a spiral staircase. But no image or "clipart" or photo captured what I felt the Lord was showing me. I wanted to capture the cycling of spiritual seasons and the growth that we incur throughout our walk with God within the staircase. As I prayed, I felt the Lord prompting me to call Alison. I called and she was excited about the idea of reading the conclusion and drawing up what the Lord would show her. Within hours of the phone call, Alison sent me several sketches, but we BOTH knew this one was it.

I am so honored to know people with different gifts that can capture the fullness of how God reveals and expresses Himself. Thank you Alison for sharing your gift with me and with the readers.

A Note from Alison:

As a tiny child, I fell in love with drawing before I knew how to write or spell. Even before I knew Jesus, my art was always somewhat dream-like. In my early 20s, I started making paintings that seemed to foreshadow future events in my life, almost like warnings and yet also like bread crumbs to show me where I'd been emotionally and spiritually. I wasn't thinking through the content or meaning behind the paintings or images as I developed them. The visual decisions I made were more intuitive and I felt as though I wasn't making art alone—art felt more like a dialogue than a monologue. Now in my 40s, I look back on my life and can see how God used art to woo me when I was younger and show me how real He is. After I became a Christian, God increased the anointing of this gift for prophetic art. Right before I met Lisa, I had actually been struggling with fear in this area. God had started talking to me about world events, and I was afraid to finish paintings—afraid of the responsibility and also afraid of failure. After Lisa prayed for me, there was a major shift in my life and I started to receive images and words of knowledge for other people. It's something that I'm still learning about and I am discovering the 'bigness' of how the Holy Spirit moves; there is no formula for His ways. As I walk out the mystery of this gift, I know in my heart that God is calling artists, poets, musicians, and creatives of all kinds to arise and shine forth His light. He longs to communicate His love, truth, hope, joy, and wisdom to the world, and He wants to co-labor with us to speak. What a gift that is! He is so gracious in His invitation to co-create with Him. If you feel called in this area, I would encourage you to obey the call and step out in faith. I promise that you will be glad you did!

For more information about Alison and her art, you can go to her website: www.alisonshepard.com

To order archival giclee prints of Alison's paintings, visit her portfolio:
http://fineartamerica.com/profiles/alison-shepard.html